Baby Gifts to Knit

Over 60 Sweet and Soft Patterns for Baby's
First Two Years

TRAFALGAR SQUARE
North Pomfret, Vermont

First published in the United States of America
in 2014 by
Trafalgar Square Books
North Pomfret, Vermont 05053

Originally published in French as *Cadeaux de naissance*.

Copyright © 2012 by Éditions Marie Claire–Société d'Information et
de Créations (SIC)
English translation © 2014 Trafalgar Square Books

ISBN: 978-1-57076-684-8

Library of Congress Control Number: 2013957009

Translation by Constance Burmeister

Printed in China

Charts/Schematics: Yolaine Fournie, Renée Méry, Olivier Ribailler
Photography: Pierre Nicou
Graphic design: Either Studio
English Technical Editor: Carol Huebscher Rhoades

10 9 8 7 6 5 4 3 2 1

Baby Gifts to Knit

Contents

*Pretty white stitches,
stylish outfits for
important days…*

1 - *Baby Bonnet*

Delicate, it is tied with a satin ribbon. With lace and crocheted picot details. Phil Coton 3 yarn. U.S. size 2-3 / 3 mm needles and U.S. size 0 / 2 mm crochet hook.

2 - *Sweater*

Play of lace and crocheted picot details. With white satin ribbon. Phil Coton 3 yarn, U.S size 2-3 / 3 mm needles and U.S. size 0 / 2 mm crochet hook.

1 - Baby Bonnet

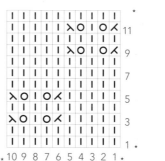

ONE SIZE

1 to 6 months

MATERIALS

Yarn: CYCA #1, Phildar Phil Coton 3 (100% Cotton, 132 yd/121 m / 50 g), 1 ball White

Needles: U.S. size 2-3 / 3 mm

Crochet hook: U.S. size 0 / 2 mm

Notions: 24 in / 60 cm white satin ribbon, ⅜ in / 1 cm wide

GAUGE

27 sts and 35 rows in lace pattern = 4 x 4 in / 10 x 10 cm. Adjust needle size to obtain gauge if necessary.

PATTERN STITCHES

Knitting:

-Garter st: Knit every row

-Lace: Repeat the 10 sts and 12 rows of the chart, making sure that each yo is accompanied by a decrease. If you cannot work both the decrease and the yarnover, work those sts in stockinette st instead.

Crochet:

-Chain (ch)

-Slip st (sl st): Insert hook into a st, yarn over and draw it through the loop on the hook

INSTRUCTIONS

The bonnet is knit in one piece, beginning with the band around the face. CO 95 sts. Knit 1 row on WS and then continue in the lace pattern, beginning with the first st of the chart. All odd-numbered rows on the chart (RS) are read from right to left; purl across on all even-numbered rows (WS).

When piece measures 5¼ in / 13 cm from cast-on row, BO 33 sts at the beg of each of the next 2 rows. Continue the lace pattern as established on the 29 center sts, decreasing 1 st at each side every 8th row 4 times. BO the 21 rem sts when piece is 9¾ in / 25 cm long.

FINISHING

Sew the back of the bonnet as indicated by the arrows on the schematic. Crochet 1 row of picots along the seam as follows: *3 sl sts, ch 3, 1 sl st into the 1st ch*. Repeat from * to *.

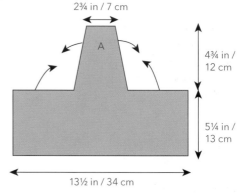

LACE PATTERN

Repeat from * to *

| = Knit on RS, purl on WS

O = Yo

⅄ = Ssk

⋋ = K2tog

Edging: Pick up and knit 82 sts along the bottom of the bonnet. Knit 11 rows of garter st. *At the same time*, on Row 1, k2tog 5 times evenly spaced over the sts of A (see schematic), and, on the 6th row, create eyelets as follows: *k4, yo, k2tog*. Repeat from * to *, ending k4. BO on Row 12.

Thread the ribbon through the eyelets.

2 - Sweater

SIZES

1 (3, 6) months

MATERIALS

Yarn: CYCA #1, Phildar Phil Coton 3 (100% Cotton, 132 yd/121 m / 50 g), 2 (2, 3) balls White

Needles: U.S. size 2-3 / 3 mm

Crochet hook: U.S. size 0 / 2 mm

Notions: 24 in / 60 cm of white satin ribbon, ⅜ in / 1 cm wide

GAUGE

27 sts and 35 rows in lace pattern = 4 x 4 in / 10 x 10 cm. Adjust needle size to obtain gauge if necessary.

PATTERN STITCHES

Knitting:

-Lace: Repeat the 12 sts and 28 rows of the chart, making sure that each yo is accompanied by a decrease on the edges of the work. If you cannot work both the decrease and the yarnover, work those sts in stockinette st instead. All odd-numbered rows on the chart (RS) are read from right to left; purl across on all even-numbered rows (WS).

Crochet:

-Chain st (ch)

-Slip st (sl st): Insert hook into a st, yarn over and draw it through the loop on the hook

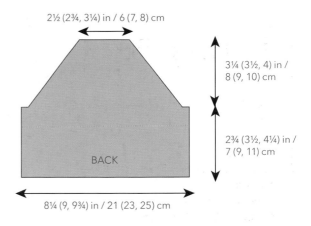

2½ (2¾, 3¼) in / 6 (7, 8) cm

3¼ (3½, 4) in / 8 (9, 10) cm

2¾ (3½, 4¼) in / 7 (9, 11) cm

BACK

8¼ (9, 9¾) in / 21 (23, 25) cm

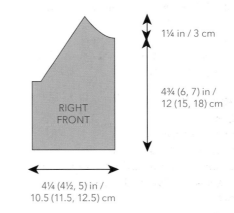

1¼ in / 3 cm

4¾ (6, 7) in / 12 (15, 18) cm

RIGHT FRONT

4¼ (4½, 5) in / 10.5 (11.5, 12.5) cm

INSTRUCTIONS

Back: CO 59 (65, 71) sts. Knit 1 row on the WS. Continue in lace pattern, beg with 10th (7th, 4th) st of chart Row 1. When piece measures 2¾ (3½, 4¼) in / 7 (9, 11) cm from cast-on row, shape the armholes by first binding off 2 sts at each side, then dec at each side: *1 st once and 2 sts once*; work * to * a total of 6 times, then dec 1 st 1 (3, 5) times. When piece measures 6 (7, 8¼) in / 15 (18, 21) cm from cast-on row, BO rem 17 (19, 21) sts.

Right Front: CO 30 (33, 36) sts. Knit 1 row on the WS. Continue in lace pattern, beg with 1st st of chart Row 1. When piece measures 2¾ (3½, 4¼) in / 7 (9, 11) cm from cast-on row, shape the armhole on the left side as for the back. When piece measures 4¾ (6, 7) in / 12 (15, 18) cm from cast-on row, shape the neck, binding off every other row at the right, 3 (4, 5) sts once, and then 1 st 4 times. When piece measures 6 (7, 8¼) in / 15 (18, 21) cm from cast-on row, BO the 2 rem sts.

Left Front: Work as for right front, reversing all shaping.

Sweater (cont.)

Sleeves (make both alike): CO 37 (43, 49) sts and knit 1 row on the WS. Continue in lace pattern, beg with 7th (4th, 1st) st of chart Row 1. When piece measures 1¼ (1¾, 2) in / 3 (4, 5) cm from cast-on row, shape sleeve cap: bind off 2 sts at each side on all sizes. Continue decreasing as follows:

1 month: Dec 1 st every other row 2 times, (work 2 rows and then dec 1 st, work 1 row and dec 1 st) 3 times, work 2 rows and then dec 1 st every other row 2 times.

3 months: Dec 1 st every other row 10 times, 1 st every 4 rows 2 times and 1 st after 2 rows once.

6 months: Dec 1 st every other row 15 times and 1 st after 4 rows once. When piece measures 4¼ (5¼, 6) in / 11 (13, 15) cm, BO the 13 rem sts.

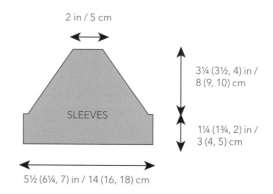

2 in / 5 cm

3¼ (3½, 4) in / 8 (9, 10) cm

SLEEVES

1¼ (1¾, 2) in / 3 (4, 5) cm

5½ (6¼, 7) in / 14 (16, 18) cm

FINISHING

Sew the armhole, sleeve, and side seams. **Bands:** Pick up and knit 33 (40, 47) sts at the right front edge, 56 (60, 64) sts around the neck, and 33 (40, 47) sts at the left front edge = 122 (140, 158) sts total. Immediately BO knitwise on WS of the work. Crochet 1 row of picots around the neck and at the edge of the sleeves as follows: *Sl 2, ch 3, sl 1 st in the first ch*; repeat from * to * around.

Cut the ribbon into 2 equal lengths and sew one at each side of the neck.

Repeat from * to *

I	= Knit on RS, purl on WS
O	= Yo
⋉	= K2tog
⋌	= Ssk

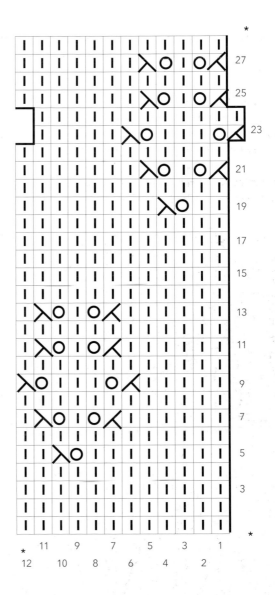

3 - Booties and Bag

Little booties and a pretty bag for storing them, all knit in lace. Yarn Phil Coton 3, needles U.S. size 2-3 / 3 mm.

4 - Dress

A play of stitches and eyelets form geometric motifs, accented with a satin ribbon. Neck details of crocheted shells and picot stitches. Phil Coton 3 yarn. U.S. sizes 1-2, 2-3, and 4 / 2.5, 3, and 3.5 mm needles and U.S. size 0 / 2 mm crochet hook.

3 - Booties and Bag

SIZE

Newborn to 3 months

MATERIALS

Yarn: CYCA #1, Phildar Phil Coton 3 (100% Cotton, 132 yd/121 m / 50 g), 1 ball White

Needles: U.S. size 2-3 / 3 mm

Notions: white satin ribbon, ⅜ in / 1 cm wide, 20 in / 50 cm each for bag and booties

GAUGE

27 sts and 35 rows in lace pattern = 4 x 4 in / 10 x 10 cm. Adjust needle size if necessary to obtain gauge.

PATTERN STITCHES

-Stockinette st: Knit on RS, purl on WS
-Lace: Follow the chart, repeating the 6 sts and 8 rows between *

LACE

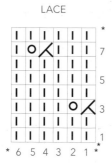

Repeat from * to *

BAG INSTRUCTIONS

CO 83 sts. Follow the chart beginning with the 3rd st of Row 3.
When piece measures 6 in / 15 cm from the cast-on row, purl 1 row on RS, work in St st for 8 rows, knit 1 row on WS, work in St st for 8 rows and then BO.

FINISHING

Fold the knitting in half to sew the side, leaving the 8 rows open between the 2 garter ridges at the top. Sew the bottom of the bag. Turn bag inside out. Fold the top at the last garter st ridge, and sew down with slip stitches. Thread the ribbon through the opening.

BOOTIE INSTRUCTIONS

Sole: CO 5 sts and work in St st, increasing 1 st at each side on the 2nd, 4th, 6th, and 10th rows. When piece measures 2½ in / 6 cm from cast-on row, dec 1 st at each side. Work 4 rows and then dec 1 st every other row 2 times. Bind off.

Foot: CO 63 sts and knit 1 row on WS. Work 7 rows in St st, making a row of eyelets on the 4th row as follows: *k2, yo, k2tog*; repeat from * to * across. Knit one row on the WS. Begin the top of the foot as follows: BO the first 9 sts (heel). Continue on the next 16 sts (side), decreasing 1 st at each side on the 2nd, 4th, 6th, and 7th rows. *At the same time*, on Row 5, make an eyelet 1 st from the each side as follows: K1, yo, k2tog, k6, k2tog, yo, k1. BO the 8 rem sts. Continue working the next 13 center sts for the tongue in St st, working the lace motif on the 5 center sts for the first 3 rows. BO purlwise on row 13 (RS). Work the rem 25 sts as for the first 25, reversing shaping.

FINISHING

Pick up and knit 20 sts around each side. On the next (WS) row, BO knitwise.
Sew the heel. Pin and sew the sole in place, with the cast-on row meeting the center of heel and the bind-off row at the toe. Cut the ribbon in half and thread one piece of ribbon through the eyelets of the sides to tie the bow on top.

MOTIF FOR THE TOP OF THE BOOTIES

Repeat from * to *

☐ = Knit on RS, purl on WS

☒ = K2tog

☒ = Ssk

4 - Dress

SIZES

1 month (6 months)

MATERIALS

Yarn: CYCA #1, Phildar Phil Coton 3 (100% Cotton, 132 yd/121 m / 50 g), 3 (4) balls White
Needles: U.S. sizes 1-2, 2-3, and 4 / 2.5, 3, and 3.5 mm
Crochet hook: U.S. size 0 / 2 mm
Notions: 35½ in / 90 cm white satin ribbon, ⅜ in / 1 cm wide; one snap

GAUGE

27 sts and 35 rows on needles U.S. size 2-3 / 3 mm = 4 x 4 in / 10 x 10 cm. Adjust needle sizes to obtain gauge if necessary.

PATTERN STITCHES

Knitting:
-Garter st: Knit every row
-Stockinette st: Knit on RS, purl on WS
-Lace: Work the 10 rows of the chart, repeating the 12 sts
-Armhole decreases: Worked on the RS. To dec one st at the beg of the row, k1, k2tog and at the end of the row, when 3 sts rem, ssk, k1. To work double dec at the beg of the row, k1, k3tog and, at the end of the row, when 4 sts rem, sl 1, k2tog, psso, k1.

Crochet:
-Slip st (sl st): Insert hook into a st, yarn over and draw it through the loop on the hook
-Double crochet (dc): Yo, insert hook into a st; yo a second time, draw yarn through st; yo and draw yarn through first 2 loops on the hook, yo and draw yarn through rem 2 loops on the hook.

Dress (cont.)

INSTRUCTIONS

Back: With U.S size 2-3 / 3 mm needles, cast on 77 (89) sts. Work 4 rows in garter st and then 10 rows of lace following the chart. Begin with the 5th st of the chart, replacing the 1st and last double decrease by a single dec (the first st of the chart). Dec 1 st every 10 (12) rows 8 times = 61 (73) sts rem.

Continue in St st after Row 6 (8) of the lace pattern.

When piece measures 9 (11¾) in / 23 (30) cm from cast-on row, work 1 row of eyelets as follows: *k2, yo, k2tog, k2*; rep from * to * across.

When piece measures 9¾ (12½) in / 24.5 (31.5) cm from cast-on row, begin the armhole shaping. BO 2 sts at each side then dec every other row as follows: BO (1 st once, 2 sts once) 5 times, and then dec 1 st 4 (7) times.

At the same time, with the first dec of 1 st, divide the work into 2 parts, binding off the center st for the slit. Finish each side separately.

When the piece measures 13 (16½) in / 33 (42) cm from cast-on row, BO the 9 (12) neck sts.

LACE CHART FOR DRESS

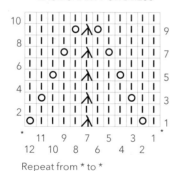

Repeat from * to *

⬛ **I** = Knit on RS, purl on WS

⬛ **O** = Yo

⬛ **⋀** = Sl 1 kwise, k2tog, psso = double decrease

Front: Work as for the back, eliminating the slit.
With the last dec of 2 sts, BO the 7 (13) center sts and finish each side separately, shaping neck neck every other row as follows: BO 2 sts once, 1 st 2 times, and 2 sts once.

Sleeves (make both alike): With U.S. size 2-3 / 3 mm needles, CO 47 (57) sts. Work 4 rows of garter st and then continue in St st. When piece measures 1 (1¾) in / 2.5 (4.5) cm from cast-on row, shape sleeve cap. BO 2 sts at each side, then on every other row, dec at each side as follows:
1 month: (1 st once, 2 sts once) 2 times and then dec 1 st 10 times.
6 months: (1 st once, 2 sts once) 4 times and then dec 1 st 9 times.
Both sizes: BO rem 11 sts.

FINISHING

Edgings on back slit: With U.S. size 1-2 / 2.5 mm needles, pick up and knit 20 (26) sts along one edge of the slit. Knit 3 garter st rows and BO. Rep along opposite edge. Overlap and sew down the 2 edgings at base of slit. Attach sleeves. Sew the sleeve and side seams.

Neckband: With U.S. size 1-2 / 2.5 mm needles, pick up and knit 54 (66) sts around the neck. Knit one row on the WS and then BO with U.S. size 4 / 3.5 mm needles. Crochet one row of shells on the BO row as follows: *Sl 1 in one st, skip one st, 4 dc in the next st, skip 1 st*; rep from * to * around. Sew on the snap to close the neckband.

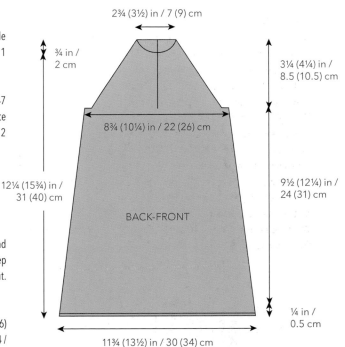

2¾ (3½) in / 7 (9) cm

¾ in / 2 cm

3¼ (4¼) in / 8.5 (10.5) cm

8¾ (10¼) in / 22 (26) cm

12¼ (15¾) in / 31 (40) cm

9½ (12¼) in / 24 (31) cm

BACK-FRONT

¼ in / 0.5 cm

11¾ (13½) in / 30 (34) cm

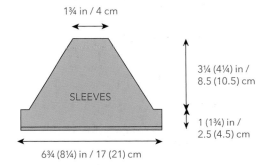

1¾ in / 4 cm

3¼ (4¼) in / 8.5 (10.5) cm

SLEEVES

1 (1¾) in / 2.5 (4.5) cm

6¾ (8¼) in / 17 (21) cm

5 & 6 - *Sweater and Diaper Cover*

An adorable vintage-style outfit, knit in stockinette stitch with ribbing details and satin ribbons. Super Baby yarn. U.S. sizes 1-2 and 2-3 / 2.5 and 3 mm needles.

7 - *Blanket*

For the cradle, buggy, stroller, knit in stockinette stitch with eyelets, cables and crocheted picot details. Aviso yarn. U.S. size 6 / 4 mm needles and U.S. size 7 / 4.5 mm crochet hook.

5 - Asymmetrical Sweater

SIZES

1 (3, 6) months

MATERIALS

Yarn: CYCA #1, Phildar Super Baby (70% Acrylic, 30% Wool, 117 yd/107 m / 25 g), 3 (4, 4) balls Swan

Needles: U.S. sizes 1-2 and 2-3 / 2.5 and 3 mm

Notions: 3 small buttons; white satin ribbon 29½ (33½, 37½) in / 75 (85, 95) cm long and ⅜ in / 1 cm wide

GAUGE

29 sts and 40 rows on larger needles = 4 x 4 in / 10 x 10 cm in St st. Adjust needle sizes to obtain gauge if necessary.

PATTERN STITCHES

-Ribbing: K2, p2
-Stockinette st: Knit on RS, purl on WS
-Eyelets: (K2tog, yo, k6)

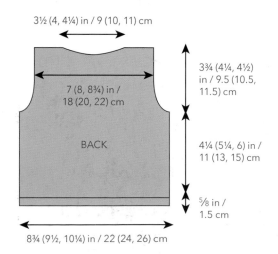

3½ (4, 4¼) in / 9 (10, 11) cm

7 (8, 8¾) in / 18 (20, 22) cm

BACK

3¾ (4¼, 4½) in / 9.5 (10.5, 11.5) cm

4¼ (5¼, 6) in / 11 (13, 15) cm

⅝ in / 1.5 cm

8¾ (9½, 10¼) in / 22 (24, 26) cm

INSTRUCTIONS

Back: With smaller needles, cast on 66 (70, 78) sts and work in k2, p2 ribbing for ⅝ in / 1.5 cm, beg with p2. Change to larger needles and work in St st, increasing 0 (2, 0) sts on the first row = 66 (72, 78) sts.

When piece measures 4½ (5¼, 6¼) in / 11.5 (13.5, 15.5) cm from cast-on row, make a row of eyelets as follows: K4 (7, 2) sts, then *k2tog on the RS, yo, k6*. Repeat from * to * across and end with k2tog, yo, k4 (7, 2).

When piece measures 5 (5¾, 6½) in / 12.5 (14.5, 16.5) cm from cast-on row, shape armholes by first binding off 2 sts at each side, and then dec 1 st at each side on every other row 4 times = 54 (60, 66) sts.

When piece measures 8¼ (9½, 10¾) in / 21 (24, 27) cm from cast-on row, BO the 14 (16, 18) center sts and work each side separately. Work 2 rows and then BO 6 sts at neck edge on next row.

When piece measures 8¾ (9¾, 11) in / 22 (25, 28) cm from cast-on row, BO the rem 14 (16, 18) sts for shoulder. Work the other shoulder the same way, reversing shaping.

Right Front: With smaller needles, cast on 57 (61, 65) sts. Work in k2, p2 ribbing for ⅝ in / 1.5 cm, beg with k3. Change to larger needles and work in St st, decreasing 2 (3, 4) sts evenly spaced across first row = 55 (58, 61) sts.

When piece measures 4½ (5¼, 6¼) in / 11.5 (13.5, 15.5) cm from cast-on row, make a row of eyelets beg with k1 (7, 3) (see Pattern Stitches).

When piece measures 4¾ (6, 7) in / 12 (15, 18) cm from cast-on row, mark the 10 (11, 12) sts, 17 sts from the right edge. Dec 1 st at the right side every other row 12 times. *At the same time,* when piece measures 5 (5¾, 6½) in / 12.5 (14.5, 16.5) cm from cast-on row, shape armhole at the left side as for the back. When piece measures 7 (8¼, 9½) in / 18 (21, 24) cm from cast-on row, BO the 10 (11, 12) marked sts. Continue working the sts at the left, binding off at the neck edge every other row as follows: 3 sts once, 2 sts once, and 1 st 2 times. Then, after 4 rows, BO 1 st.

When piece measures 8¾ (9¾, 11) in / 22 (25, 28) cm from cast-on row, BO 14 (16, 18) sts for the shoulder. Continue working the 5 rem sts on the right and BO every other row for the neck: 3 sts once and 2 sts once.

Left Front: With smaller needles, cast on 25 (29, 33) sts. Beginning with p1, work k2, p2 ribbing for ⅝ in / 1.5 cm. Change to larger needles and continue in St st, decreasing 1 (2, 3) sts evenly spaced across first row = 24 (27, 30) sts.

When piece measures 4½ (5¼, 6¼) in / 11.5 (13.5, 15.5) cm from cast-on row, make a row of eyelets as for the back.

When piece measures 5 (5¾, 6½) in / 12.5 (14.5, 16.5) cm from cast-on row, shape armhole on the right side as for the back.

When piece measures 7 (8¼, 9½) in / 18 (21, 24) cm from cast-on row, shape neck on the left side by binding off on every other row: 2 (3, 4) sts once and 1 st once. Then work 4 rows and BO 1 st.

When piece measures 8¾ (9¾, 11) in / 22 (25, 28) cm from cast-on row, BO rem 14 (16, 18) sts for shoulder.

Sleeves (make both alike): With smaller needles, CO 46 (50, 54) sts. Work in k2, p2 ribbing for ⅝ in / 1.5 cm. Change to larger needles and continue in St st, decreasing 2 sts evenly spaced across first row = 44 (48, 52) sts.

Inc at each side as follows: 1 st every 5th row 7 times (1 st every 6th row 8 times, 1 st every 6th row 9 times) = 58 (64, 70) sts.

When piece measures 4¼ (6, 6¾) in / 11 (15, 17) cm from cast-on row, BO 1 st at each side on every other row 4 times and then 2 sts once. BO rem sts.

FINISHING

Sew the shoulder seams.

Neckband: With smaller needles, pick up and knit 76 (80, 84) sts around the neck. Work 7 rows of k2, p2 ribbing, beginning and ending with k3. BO.

Right front band: With smaller needles, pick up and knit 72 (84, 96) sts and work as for the neckband, making 3 one-stitch buttonholes (yo, k2tog) on the 4th row. The first buttonhole should be at the base of the diagonal, one at the middle of the diagonal, and the third 3 sts from the neck edge.

Left front band: With smaller needles, pick up and knit 68 (80, 92) sts and work as for the neck/right front band, omitting the buttonholes.

Attach sleeves. Sew the sleeve and side seams. Overlap the fronts, right over left, and sew on the buttons. Thread the ribbon through the eyelets and tie over the ribbing of the front bands.

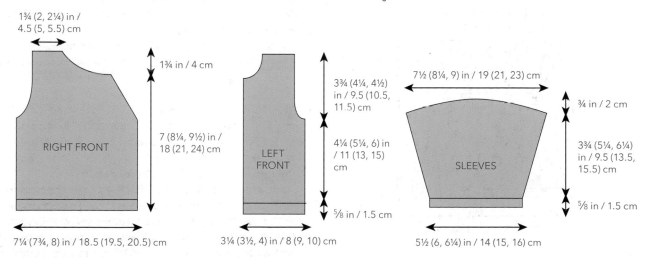

RIGHT FRONT

1¾ (2, 2¼) in / 4.5 (5, 5.5) cm

1¾ in / 4 cm

7 (8¼, 9½) in / 18 (21, 24) cm

7¼ (7¾, 8) in / 18.5 (19.5, 20.5) cm

LEFT FRONT

3¾ (4¼, 4½) in / 9.5 (10.5, 11.5) cm

4¼ (5¼, 6) in / 11 (13, 15) cm

⅝ in / 1.5 cm

3¼ (3½, 4) in / 8 (9, 10) cm

SLEEVES

7½ (8¼, 9) in / 19 (21, 23) cm

¾ in / 2 cm

3¾ (5¼, 6¼) in / 9.5 (13.5, 15.5) cm

⅝ in / 1.5 cm

5½ (6, 6¼) in / 14 (15, 16) cm

6 - Diaper Cover

SIZES
1 (3, 6) months

MATERIALS
Yarn: CYCA #1, Phildar Super Baby (70% Acrylic, 30% Wool, 117 yds/107 m / 25 g), 2 (4, 4) balls White

Needles: U.S. size 1-2 and 2-3 / 2.5 and 3 mm.

Notions: 3 small buttons; white satin ribbon 27½ (31½, 35½) in / 70 (80, 90) cm long and ³⁄₈ in / 1 cm wide

GAUGE
29 sts and 40 rows on larger needles = 4 x 4 in / 10 cm in St st. Adjust needle sizes if necessary to obtain gauge.

PATTERN STITCHES
-Ribbing: K2, p2

-Stockinette st: Knit on RS, purl on WS

-Eyelets: *P2tog, yo, work 6 sts in ribbing*; rep * to *

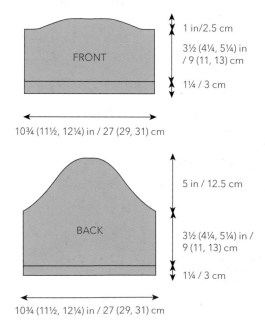

FRONT

1 in/2.5 cm

3½ (4¼, 5¼) in / 9 (11, 13) cm

1¼ / 3 cm

10¾ (11½, 12¼) in / 27 (29, 31) cm

BACK

5 in / 12.5 cm

3½ (4¼, 5¼) in / 9 (11, 13) cm

1¼ / 3 cm

10¾ (11½, 12¼) in / 27 (29, 31) cm

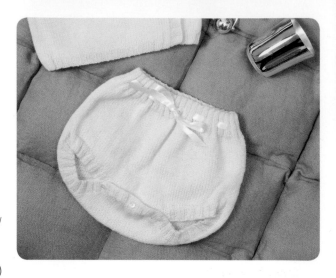

INSTRUCTIONS
Back: With smaller needles, CO 82 (86, 94) sts. Beginning with p2, work in k2, p2 ribbing for 1¼ in / 3 cm and, *at the same time*, when ribbing is half completed, make a row of eyelets as follows: Work ribbing for 4 (6, 2) sts, *p2tog, yo, work ribbing for 6 sts*. End with 4 (6, 2) sts in ribbing.

Change to larger needles and work in St st, decreasing 2 (0, 2) sts on the first row = 80 (86, 92) sts. When piece measures 4¾ (5½, 6¼) in / 12 (14, 16) cm from cast-on row, shape sides as follows:

1 month: On every other row, BO 1 st every 4 rows 2 times, then every other row 1 st 7 times, 2 sts 6 times, 1 st 6 times, 2 sts 2 times.

3 months: On every other row, BO 1 st every 4 rows 2 times, then every other row 1 st 7 times, (2 sts once, 3 sts once) 3 times, 1 st 6 times, and 2 sts 2 times.

6 months: On every other row, BO 1 st every 4 rows 2 times, then every other row 1 st 7 times, 3 sts 6 times, 1 st 6 times, 2 sts 2 times.

Bind off rem 18 sts for the crotch.

Front: Begin as for the back. When piece measures 4¾ (5½, 6¼) in / 12 (14, 16) cm from cast-on, shape sides: on every other row at each side, BO 12 (15, 18) sts once, 6 sts once, 5 sts once, and 4 sts 2 times. Bind off rem 18 sts for the crotch.

FINISHING
Band at the bottom of the back: With smaller needles, pick up and knit 110 (118, 126) sts at the bottom of the back. Work 7 rows of k2, p2 ribbing, making 3 one-st buttonholes on the 4th row–one in the center of the crotch and one 12 sts from each side. Bind off.

Band at the bottom of the front: Pick up and knit 82 (90, 98) sts and work as for the back, omitting the buttonholes.

Sew the side seams. Sew the buttons on front band. Thread the ribbon through the eyelets so that it can be tied at center front.

7 - Blanket

FINISHED MEASUREMENTS
Approx. 23¾ x 31½ in / 60 x 80 cm

MATERIALS
Yarn: CYCA #4, Phildar Aviso (60% Cotton, 40% Acrylic, 74 yd/68 m / 50 g),
8 balls White
Needles: U.S. sizes 6 and 7 / 4 and 5 mm; cable needle
Crochet hook: U.S. size 7 / 4.5 mm

GAUGE
16 sts and 23 rows in pattern on larger needles = 4 x 4 in / 10 x 10 cm.
Adjust needle sizes if necessary to obtain gauge.

PATTERN STITCHES
Knitting:
-Pattern: Follow the chart, repeating the sts and rows between *
Crochet:
-Slip st (sl st): Insert hook into a st, yarn over and draw it through the loop
on the hook
-Single crochet (sc): Insert hook into a st, yo, draw yarn through st, yo and
draw yarn through the 2 loops on the hook
-Chain (ch)

INSTRUCTIONS
Using larger needles, CO 95 sts. K1 for the edge st, repeat the 27 sts of the
chart 3 times, ending with the 12 first sts and k1 (edge st). Repeat the 8 rows
for 31½ in / 80 cm. Bind off.
With crochet hook, sl st around the blanket then crochet a round of picots as
follows: *4 sl sts, ch 3, 1 sl st into 3rd ch from hook*.

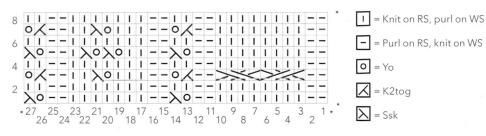

Repeat from * to *

= sl 2 sts to the cn and hold in back of
work. K2 then k2 from the cn. Sl 2 sts to
the cn and hold in front of work. K2 then
k2 from the cn.

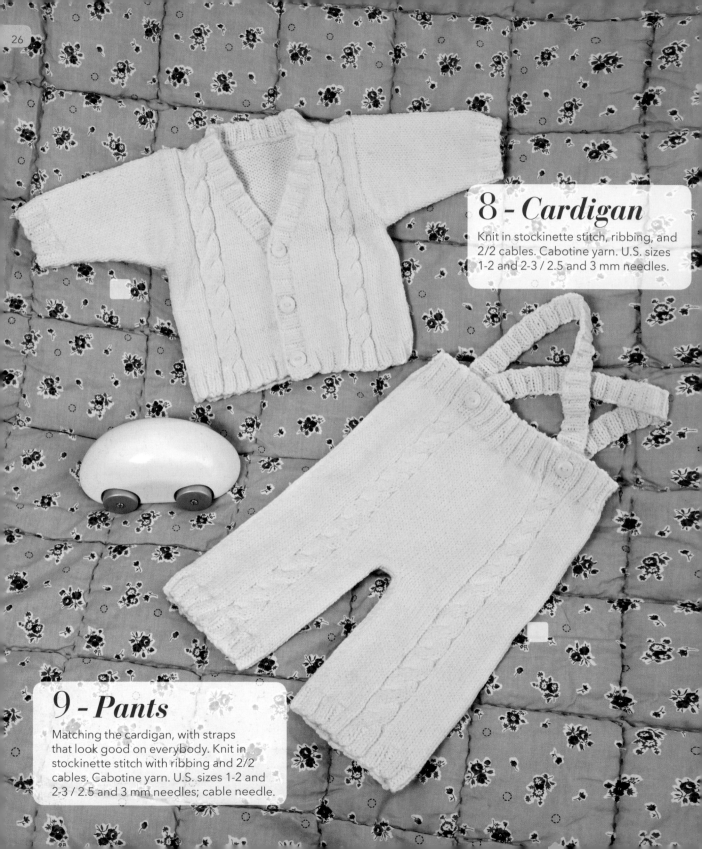

8 - Cardigan

Knit in stockinette stitch, ribbing, and 2/2 cables. Cabotine yarn. U.S. sizes 1-2 and 2-3 / 2.5 and 3 mm needles.

9 - Pants

Matching the cardigan, with straps that look good on everybody. Knit in stockinette stitch with ribbing and 2/2 cables. Cabotine yarn. U.S. sizes 1-2 and 2-3 / 2.5 and 3 mm needles; cable needle.

10 - Booties

Fitting the foot cozily, tied with a ribbon. Knit in garter stitch. Phil Coton 3 yarn. U.S. size 2-3 / 3 mm needles.

8 - Cardigan

SIZES

1 (3, 6) months

MATERIALS

Yarn: CYCA #2, Phildar Cabotine (55% Cotton, 45% Acrylic, 136 yd/124 m / 50 g), 2 (2, 3) balls White

Needles: U.S. sizes 1-2 and 2-3 / 2.5 and 3 mm; cable needle

Notions: 3 buttons; optional: stitch markers

GAUGE

26 sts and 33 rows in charted pattern on larger needles = 4 x 4 in / 10 x 10 cm. Adjust needle sizes if necessary to obtain gauge.

PATTERN STITCHES

-Ribbing: *K2, p2*
-Stockinette stitch: Knit on RS, purl on WS
-Cable: Work the 10 sts and 8 rows as shown on chart

INSTRUCTIONS

Back: With smaller needles, CO 62 (66, 74) sts. Work in k2, p2 ribbing for ¾ in / 2 cm, increasing 0 (2, 0) sts on the last row = 62 (68, 74) sts. Change to larger needles. Work 11 (13, 15) sts in St st, pm, work 10 sts following cable chart, pm, work 20 (22, 24) sts in St st, pm, 10 sts cable, pm, work 11 (13, 15) sts in St st.

When piece measures 5¼ (6, 6¾) in / 13 (15, 17) cm from cast-on row, shape armholes at each side on every other row as follows: BO 2 sts once and 1 st 4 times = 50 (56, 62) sts.

When piece measures 8¾ (9¾, 11) in / 22 (25, 28) cm from cast-on row, BO the center 12 (14, 16) sts and work each side separately. Work 2 rows, then BO 6 sts at the neck.

When piece measures 9 (10¼, 11½) in / 23 (26, 29) cm from cast-on row, BO the rem 13 (15, 17) sts for shoulder. Work the other side the same way, reversing shaping.

Left Front: With smaller needles, CO 33 (35, 37) sts. Work ¾ in / 2 cm in k2, p2 ribbing; dec 1 st on the last row of the smallest size and inc 1 st on the last row of the largest size = 32 (35, 38) sts. Change to larger needles and work 11 (12, 13) sts in St st, pm, 10 sts following the cable chart, pm, 11 (13, 15) sts in St st.

When piece measures 5¼ (6, 6¾) in / 13 (15, 17) cm from cast-on row, shape armhole as for the back and *at the same time* dec at the left side for the neck as follows: dec 1 st every other row 13 times (1 st every other row 12 times and 1 st every 4th row 2 times; st every other row 11 times and 1 st every 4th row 4 times).

When piece measures 9 (10¼, 11½) in / 23 (26, 29) cm from cast-on row, BO rem 13 (15, 17) sts for shoulder.

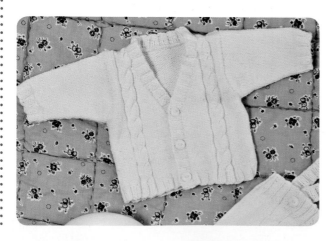

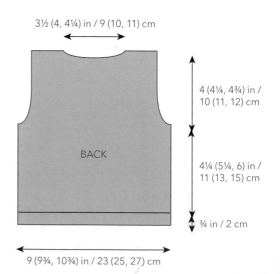

3½ (4, 4¼) in / 9 (10, 11) cm

4 (4¼, 4¾) in / 10 (11, 12) cm

BACK

4¼ (5¼, 6) in / 11 (13, 15) cm

¾ in / 2 cm

9 (9¾, 10¾) in / 23 (25, 27) cm

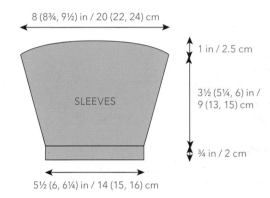

8 (8¾, 9½) in / 20 (22, 24) cm

1 in / 2.5 cm

3½ (5¼, 6) in / 9 (13, 15) cm

¾ in / 2 cm

5½ (6, 6¼) in / 14 (15, 16) cm

Right Front: Work as for left front, reversing all shaping.

Sleeves: With smaller needles, CO 38 (42, 46) sts. Work in k2, p2 ribbing for ¾ in / 2 cm. Change to larger needles. Work in St st, increasing at each side as follows: inc 1 st every 4 rows 7 times (1 st every 5 rows 8 times, 1 st every 5 rows 9 times) = 52 (58, 64) sts.

When piece measures 4¼ (6, 6¾) in / 11 (15, 17) cm from cast-on row, shape sleeve cap: at each side, on every other row, BO 2 sts once and 1 st 4 times. BO rem sts.

FINISHING

Sew the shoulder seams.

Bands: With smaller needles, pick up and knit 33 (38, 44) sts along edge of the right front, 35 (38, 41) sts along the diagonal of right front neck, 28 (30, 32) sts along back neck, 35 (38, 41) sts along the diagonal of left front neck, and 33 (38, 44) sts down the left front edge = 164 (182, 202) sts. Beginning and ending with k3, work 7 rows of k2, p2 ribbing. *At the same time*, on Row 4, make 3 one-stitch buttonholes; one should be placed 4 sts from the bottom and the others spaced 12 (14, 16) sts apart. Bind off.

Sew in the sleeves. Sew the sleeve and side seams. Sew on the buttons.

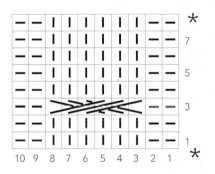

Repeat from * to *

| I | = Knit on RS, purl on WS

| − | = Purl on RS, knit on WS

= Sl 3 sts to the cn and hold in back of work. K3, then k3 from the cn.

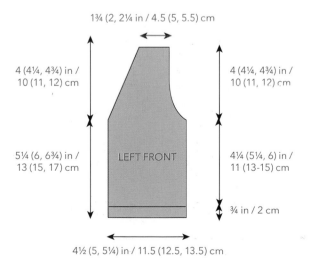

1¾ (2, 2¼ in / 4.5 (5, 5.5) cm

4 (4¼, 4¾) in / 10 (11, 12) cm

4 (4¼, 4¾) in / 10 (11, 12) cm

LEFT FRONT

5¼ (6, 6¾) in / 13 (15, 17) cm

4¼ (5¼, 6) in / 11 (13-15) cm

¾ in / 2 cm

4½ (5, 5¼) in / 11.5 (12.5, 13.5) cm

9 - Pants

SIZES
1 (3, 6) months

MATERIALS
Yarn: CYCA #2, Phildar Cabotine (55% Cotton, 45% Acrylic, 136 yd/124m / 50 g), 2 (2, 3) balls White

Needles: U.S. sizes 1-2 and 2-3 / 2.5 and 3 mm; cable needle

Notions: 2 buttons; stitch markers; stitch holder

GAUGE
26 sts and 33 rows in pattern on larger needles = 4 x 4 in / 10 x 10 cm. Adjust needle sizes if necessary to obtain gauge.

PATTERN STITCHES
-Ribbing: K2, p2
-Stockinette st: Knit on RS, purl on WS
-Cable: Work the 10 sts and 8 rows of the chart

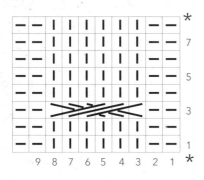

Repeat from * to *

| I | = Knit on RS and purl on WS

| – | = Purl on RS and knit on WS

= Sl 3 sts to cn and hold in back of work; k3, then k3 from cn.

INSTRUCTIONS

Back: With smaller needles, CO 34 (38, 42) sts for the bottom of the left leg. Work in k2, p2 ribbing for ¾ in / 2 cm, decreasing 0 (1, 2) sts on the last row = 34 (37, 40) sts. Change to larger needles and work in St st for 11 (12, 13) sts (center of pants), pm, work Row 1 of the chart over 10 sts, pm, work rem 13 (15, 17) sts in St st (at the side). Place all sts on a holder when piece measures 5½ (7, 8¼) in / 14 (18, 21) cm from cast-on row. Knit the right leg, reversing the shaping. CO 2 sts for the crotch and continue working in pattern on all 70 (76, 82) sts. When piece measures 11½, (13½, 15) in / 29 (34, 38) cm from cast-on row, change to smaller needles to work the waist. Work k2, p2 ribbing for 1¼ in / 3 cm beginning and ending the first row with k2 and decreasing 0 (2, 0) sts on that row. Bind off.

Front: Work as for the back, making a one-st buttonhole above each cable midway through the waist ribbing.

Straps: With larger needles, CO 92 (104, 116) sts. Work 6 rows of k2, p2 ribbing and bind off.

FINISHING
Sew the side and crotch seams. Sew the straps to the back. Sew a button onto each strap.

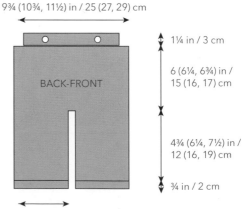

9¾ (10¾, 11½) in / 25 (27, 29) cm

BACK-FRONT

1¼ in / 3 cm

6 (6¼, 6¾) in / 15 (16, 17) cm

4¾ (6¼, 7½) in / 12 (16, 19) cm

¾ in / 2 cm

4¾ (5¼, 5½) in / 12 (13, 14) cm

10 - *Booties*

SIZE
Newborn to 3 months

MATERIALS
Yarn: CYCA #1, Phildar Phil Coton 3 (100% Cotton, 132 yd/121 m / 50 g),
1 ball White
Needles: U.S. size 2-3 / 3 mm
Notions: white satin ribbon 31½ in / 80 cm long, ¼ in / 7 mm wide

PATTERN STITCHES
-Garter st: Knit every row

INSTRUCTIONS
The booties are made in a single piece beg with the sole. CO 11 sts and work
in garter st for 3 in / 7.5 cm. CO 24 sts at each side for the foot = 59 sts. On
the first row, knit the last st of the foot tog with the first st of the sole, and
then the last st of the sole tog with the first of the foot = 57 sts.
When piece measures 4¼ in / 10.5 cm from cast-on, work as follows: k3, yo,
k2tog, k4, yo, k2tog, k35, k2tog, yo, k4, k2tog, yo, k3.
On the next row, continue working the 9 center sts for the top of the foot
and, at the end of each row, knit one st from the top of the foot tog with one
st from the side sts 11 times. *At the same time*, on the 10th dec row, make 2
eyelets on the center 9 sts as follows: k1, yo, k2tog, k3, k2tog, yo, k1. After
the last dec row, BO all sts purlwise on the RS or knitwise on the WS.
Sew the heel. Sew the foot around the sole. Cut the ribbon in half and thread
through the eyelets in order to make a bow on the top of the foot.

*Charm and tradition
for girls and boys...*

11 & 12
Sleep Sack and Snuggly Owl

For sweet dreams, a sleep sack made in stockinette stitch with an embroidered moon. A snuggly "owl" made in stockinette and garter stitches decorated with I-cord. Phil Thalassa yarn. U.S. sizes 4 and 6 / 3.5 and 4 mm needles.

13 - *Mobile*

To place above the cradle and decorate the room, pompoms, moon, owl, star and I-cord. Made in stockinette and garter stitches. Phil Thalassa yarn. U.S. size 4 / 3.5 mm needles, U.S. size D-3 / 3 mm crochet hook, and I-cord.

11 - *Sleep Sack*

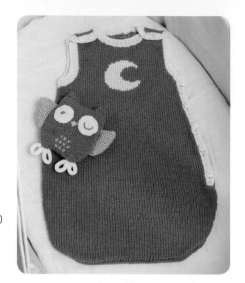

SIZE

Newborn to 6 months

MATERIALS

Yarn: CYCA #3, Phildar Phil Thalassa (75% Cotton, 25% Tencel, 88yd/80m / 50 g), 5 balls Slate and 1 ball White; scrap yarn

Needles: U.S. sizes 2-3, 4 and 6 / 3, 3.5 and 4 mm

Notions: 9 buttons; 4 snaps

GAUGE

20 sts and 28 rows on U.S. size 6 / 4 mm needles = 4 x 4 in / 10 x 10 cm. Adjust needle sizes if necessary to obtain gauge.

PATTERN STITCHES

-Ribbing: K1, p1

-Stockinette: Knit on RS, purl on WS

-Duplicate: embroidery

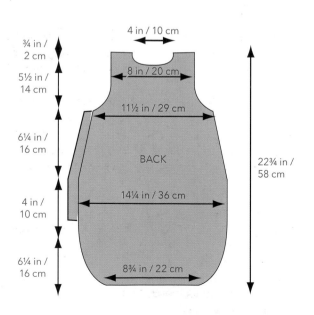

INSTRUCTIONS

Back: With U.S. size 6 / 4 mm needles and Slate, CO 46 sts. Work in St st, increasing at each side as follows: on every other row, CO 2 sts 3 times and 1 st 3 times; inc 1 st every 4th row 2 times, and 1 st every 6th row 3 times = 74 sts. When piece measures 6¼ in / 16 cm, CO 4 additional sts at the left side = 78 sts. When piece measures 10¼ in / 26 cm, work decreases as follows, always keeping 1 stitch at the right edge and 5 sts at the left edge in St st: dec 1 st, work 8 rows, dec 1 st, and every 6th row dec 1 st 5 times = 64 sts.

When piece measures 16½ in / 42 cm from cast-on row, begin the armhole shaping. BO 3 sts on the right edge and 7 sts on the left; then, at each side, BO 2 sts 2 times and 1 st 2 times = 42 sts.

When piece measures 21¾ in / 55 cm from cast-on row, shape the neck as follows: BO the 10 center sts then work each side separately. Work 2 rows and then BO 5 sts at neck edge.

When piece measures 22 in / 56 cm, mark the edge sts. When piece measures 22¾ in / 58 cm, BO the rem 11 sts for the shoulder.

Work the other side of the neck the same way, reversing shaping.

Front: With U.S. size 6 / 4 mm needles and Slate, CO 46 sts. Work in St st, increasing at each side as follows: on every other row, CO 2 sts 3 times and 1 st 3 times; inc 1 st every 4th row 2 times, and 1 st every 6th row 3 times = 74 sts. When piece measures 6¼ in / 16 cm, BO 4 sts on the right edge = 70 sts.

When piece measures 10¼ in / 26 cm, work decreases inside edge st as follows: dec 1 at each side, work 8 rows and then dec 1 at each side, and every 6th row dec 1 st at each side 5 times = 56 sts.

When piece measures 16½ in / 42 cm, mark the edge st on the right side and begin the armhole shaping as follows: BO 3 sts on the left side, work 2 rows, BO 1 st on the right side and 2 sts on the left; then, at each side, BO 2 sts once

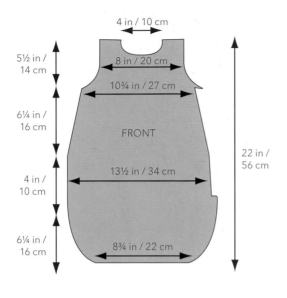

MOON CHART

= 1 st and 1 row in White

↑
Center of the piece

and 1 st 2 times = 42 sts.

When piece measures 20½ in / 52 cm, begin neck shaping: BO the 6 center sts and work each side separately. At neck edge, on every other row, BO 3 sts once, 2 sts once, and 1 st 2 times.

When piece measures 22 in / 56 cm, BO rem 11 sts for the shoulder.

Work the other side of the neck the same way, reversing shaping.

Button Band: With U.S. size 4 / 3.5 mm needles and White, CO 55 sts.

Work in k1, p1 ribbing, beginning and ending the first and third rows with k2.

Make 5 buttonholes of 2 sts each on the 3rd row, the first 4 sts from the edge and the others spaced 9 sts apart.

When band measures ¾ in / 2 cm, knit 1 row on the RS and, with scrap yarn, work a few rows of St st. Ironing these rows will help in removing them for sewing.

FINISHING

Embroider the moon in duplicate st with White, centering moon on the front at 15 in / 38 cm (see chart).

Front Details: With U.S. size 2-3 / 3 mm needles and White, pick up and knit 24 sts at the right armhole, 11 sts on the shoulder, 22 sts around the front neck, 11 sts on the 2nd shoulder and 30 sts around the left armhole = 98 sts.

Change to U.S. size 4 / 3.5 mm needles and knit one row on the WS. Then work in k1, p1 ribbing as follows: 24 sts in ribbing, M1, work 1 st, M1, 9 sts in ribbing, M1, work 1 st, M1, 22 sts in ribbing, M1, work 1 st, M1, 9 sts in ribbing, M1, work 1 st, M1 and 30 sts in ribbing. Work one row, then repeat so that the increases are above the others. When the band measures ¾ in / 2 cm, bind off all sts loosely.

Back Details: With U.S. size 2-3 / 3 mm needles and White, pick up and knit 35 sts at the right armhole, 11 sts on the shoulder, 32 sts around the back neck, 11 sts on the 2nd shoulder, and 41 sts at the left armhole = 130 sts.

Change to U.S. size 4 / 3.5 mm needles and knit one row on the WS, then work in k1, p1 ribbing as follows: 35 sts in ribbing, M1, work 1 st, M1, 9 sts in ribbing, M1, work 1 st, M1, 32 sts in ribbing, M1, work 1 st, M1, 9 sts in ribbing, M1, work 1 st, M1, and 41 sts in ribbing. Work one row, then repeat so that the increases are above the others. When the band measures ¾ in / 2 cm, bind off all sts loosely.

Sew the curve and the left side seams.

With RS facing and back stitch, sew the button band along the front and the armhole bands st by st.

Sew 5 of the buttons along the side.

Sew 2 snaps on each front shoulder band.

Sew 2 snaps under each back shoulder band.

Sew a button over each snap.

12 - *Snuggly Owl*

MATERIALS

Yarn: CYCA #3, Phildar Phil Thalassa (75% Cotton, 25% Tencel, 88 yd/80 m / 50 g), 1 ball each Slate, White, and Skyline

Needles: U.S. size 4 / 3.5 mm

Crochet hook: U.S. size D-3 / 3 mm

Notions: Stuffing material; I-cord knitting mill

PATTERN STITCHES

Knitting:

-Garter st: Knit every row

-Stockinette st: Knit on RS, purl on WS

Crochet:

-Chain st (ch)

-Slip st (sl st): Insert hook into a st, yarn over and draw it through the loop on the hook

-Single crochet (sc): Insert hook into a st, yo, draw yarn through st, yo and draw yarn through the 2 loops on the hook

Embroidery:

-Duplicate st

-Stem st, French knot, and satin st

INSTRUCTIONS

Body (make 2 alike): Knit following the owl diagram:

With Slate, CO 21 sts and work in St st, increasing at each side on every other row as follows: 1 st 3 times, and then, on every 4th row, increase 1 st 2 times = 31 sts.

On Row 24, begin shaping at each side as follows: BO 1 st once, work one row, BO 1 st once, work 3 rows, BO 1 st once, work 5 rows, BO 1 st once.

On Row 38, BO the 9 center sts then work each side separately. To shape the ear, BO 1 st at each side on every other row 2 times.

On Row 44, BO 3 rem sts.

Work the 2nd ear as for the first.

Wings: Knit following the diagram for the wings:

With Skyline, CO 42 sts. Work in garter st and BO 1 st at each side every 4 rows 5 times = 32 sts. On Row 24, mark the edge sts to indicate the fold line, then inc 1 st at each side. *At the same time,* BO the 26 center sts. Work each side separately to form the front part of the wing. At outer edge on every 4th row, increase 1 st 4 times. On Row 44 from the cast-on, BO the rem 8 sts.

OWL CHART

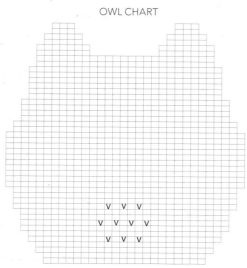

Make 2

□ = 1 st and 1 row in Slate

v = Duplicate st in Skyline

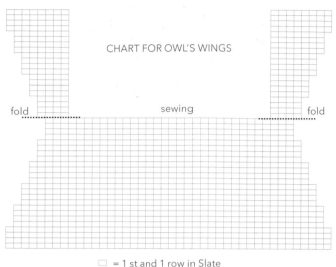

CHART FOR OWL'S WINGS

fold ┈┈┈┈┈┈   sewing   ┈┈┈┈┈┈ fold

□ = 1 st and 1 row in Slate

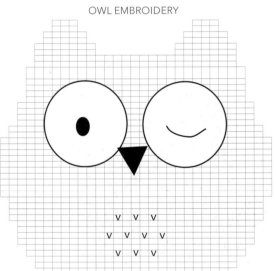

OWL EMBROIDERY

Eyes (make 2 alike): With crochet hook and White, ch 4 and close into a ring with a sl st. Work in sc as follows:

Rnd 1: Ch 1 (= 1 sc), 3 sc around ring. End rnd with 1 sl st into 1st chain st.

Rnd 2: Ch 1 (= 1 sc), 1 sc in the same st, *2 sc in each sc st of the preceding rnd*. Repeat from * to *. End rnd with 1 sl st into 1st chain st = 8 sc total.

Rnd 3: Ch 1 (= 1 sc), 1 sc in the same st, *2 sc in each sc of the preceding rnd*. Repeat from * to *. End rnd with 1 sl st into 1st chain st = 16 sc total.

Rnd 4: Ch 1 (= 1 sc), 1 sc in the same st, *2 sc in each sc of the preceding rnd*. Repeat from * to *. End rnd with 1 sl st into 1st chain st = 32 sc total.

FINISHING

With Skyline, embroider one side of the body in duplicate st (see diagram). Sew the 2 sides of the body, leaving an opening; stuff, and then sew closed. Sew the eyes on the front of the body. To sew the wings to the body, place the large straight part on the back of the owl and sew in place; fold the wings onto the front and sew the sides, leaving an opening. Stuff the wings and sew closed. Sew along the front through both thicknesses to separate the wings from the body.

Embroider the eyes with Slate. Make a French knot in the middle of one eye and embroider the other eye with stem st. Embroider the nose in satin st with Skyline.

With White, make 2 I-cords about 7 in / 18 cm long. Fold one cord to make 2 loops and attach them to the owl to form feet. Repeat with the second cord.

13 - *Mobile*

MATERIALS

Yarn: CYCA #3, Phildar Phil Thalassa (75% Cotton, 25% Tencel, 88 yd/80 m / 50 g), 1 ball each Slate, White, and Skyline

Needles: U.S. size 4 / 3.5 mm

Crochet hook: U.S. size D-3 / 3 mm

Notions: I-cord knitting mill; 15¾ in / 40 cm white twill; 1 white wooden dowel 15¾ in / 40 cm long and 5/16 in / 10 mm in diameter (similar to a curtain rod); 2 white wooden ferrules; stuffing material; stitch holder

PATTERN STITCHES

Knitting:

-Garter st: Knit every row

-Stockinette st: Knit on RS, purl on WS

Crochet:

-Chain st (ch)

-Slip st (sl st): Insert hook into a st, yarn over and draw it through the loop on the hook

-Single crochet (sc): Insert hook into a st, yo, draw yarn through st, yo, draw through the 2 loops on the hook

Embroidery:

-Duplicate st

-French knot and satin st

OWL INSTRUCTIONS

Body: Work following the chart:

With Slate, CO 19 sts, work in St st, binding off 1 st at each side every 8th row 2 times = 15 sts. On Row 24, BO the center 5 sts then work each side separately to form the ear. BO 1 st at the center of Row 26. On Row 28, BO the rem 4 sts. Make the 2nd ear the same way.

Wings: Work according to the chart as follows:

With Skyline, CO 24 sts. Work in garter st and BO 1 st at each side on Row 4 and then on every other row, BO 1 st 2 times = 18 sts.

On Row 10, mark the edge sts to indicate the fold. *At the same time*, BO the 10 center sts, then continue each side separately to make the front part of the wing. Work 2 rows and then, at outer edge, increase as follows: 1 st once, then 1 st on every other row 2 times. On Row 20, BO the rem 7 sts. Work the second side as for the first.

Eyes (make 2 alike): With White, ch 4 and join into a ring with 1 sl st. Work in sc as follows:

Rnd 1: Ch 1 (= 1 sc), 3 sc around ring. End rnd with 1 sl st into 1st chain st.

Rnd 2: Ch 1 (= 1 sc), 1 sc in the same st, *2 sc in each sc st of the preceding rnd*. Repeat from * to *. End rnd with 1 sl st into 1st chain st = 8 sc total.

OWL CHART

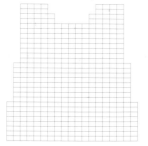

Make 2

☐ = 1 st and 1 row in Slate

EMBROIDERY CHART

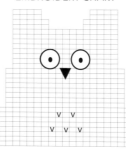

▼ = Satin st in Skyline
● = French knot in Slate
v = Duplicate st in Skyline

OWL'S WINGS CHART

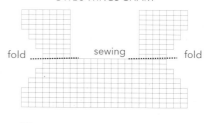

fold   sewing   fold

☐ = 1 st and 1 row in Skyline

STAR CHART

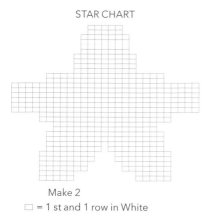

Make 2

☐ = 1 st and 1 row in White

MOON CHART

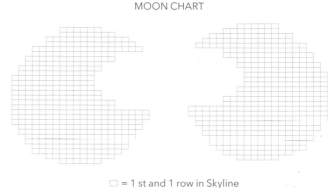

☐ = 1 st and 1 row in Skyline

STAR INSTRUCTIONS (MAKE 2 ALIKE)

With White, CO 5 sts. Work in St st for 8 rows, following the chart, and then slip sts to a holder. Make the 2nd side, reversing the shaping. Join the 2 sides, adding 1 st in the center of the work on row 9 = 17 sts. On Row 32, BO the rem 5 sts. Assemble the 2 pieces, leaving an opening. Stuff and close the opening.

MOON INSTRUCTIONS

With Skyline, CO 6 sts. Work in St st, following the chart. On Row 28, BO the rem 6 sts. Make a second piece, reversing the shaping. Assemble the 2 pieces, leaving an opening. Stuff and close the opening.

BALL INSTRUCTIONS (MAKE 2 ALIKE)

With Slate, ch 4. Work 1 sl st into first ch to form ring. Crochet around as follows:

Rnd 1: Ch 1 (= 1 sc), 3 sc around ring. Sl st 1 into the ch at the beg of rnd to close.

Rnd 2: Ch 1 (= 1 sc), 1 sc in the same st, *2 sc in each sc of the preceding rnd*; repeat from * to *. Sl st 1 into the ch at the beg of rnd to close = 8 sc.

Rnd 3: Ch 1 (= 1 sc), 1 sc in the same st, *2 sc in each sc of the preceding rnd*; repeat from * to *. Sl st 1 into the ch at the beg of rnd to close = 16 sc.

Rnds 4, 5, 6, and 7: Ch 1 (= 1 sc), 1 sc in each sc of the preceding rnd. Sl st 1 into the ch at the beg of rnd to close.

Rnd 8: Ch 1 (= 1 sc), 1 sc in the same st, BO, *sc 2 tog*; repeat from * to *. Sl st 1 into the ch at the beg of rnd to close = 8 sc. Stuff the ball.

Rnd 9: Ch 1 (= 1 sc), 1 sc in the same st, BO, *sc 2 tog*; repeat from * to *. Sl st 1 into the ch at the beg of rnd to close = 4 sc.

Cut yarn and thread through rem sts, pulling snugly.

FINISHING

With Skyline, embroider one piece of the owl's body in duplicate st (see chart). Assemble the 2 pieces of the body, leaving an opening; stuff and close. To sew the wings to the body, place the large straight part on the back of the owl and sew in place; fold the wings to the front and sew the sides. Sew the eyes onto the front of the body. Embroider the eyes, making one French knot in Slate in the middle. With Skyline, embroider the nose in satin st. With White, make 2 I cords, each about 5½ in / 14 cm long.

Fold 1 cord, forming 2 loops, and sew in place for the owl's foot. Repeat with the 2nd cord.

Cut 5½ in / 14 cm of twill and sew one side between the owl's ears. Fold the other side to form a loop of 2¾ in / 7 cm and sew. Make 2 pompoms about 1¾ in / 4 cm in diameter (1 in Horizon and 1 in White). Cut a 5¼ in / 13 cm length of twill and sew one side at the top of the moon. Fold the other side to form a loop of 2¾ in / 7 cm and sew. Attach the White pompom below the moon. With White, crochet a chain of 1¾ in / 4.5 cm to attach the White pompom to the crocheted ball.

Sew the rem twill onto a crocheted ball; fold the other end to form a loop of 2¾ in / 7 cm and sew. With White, crochet a chain of 1¾ in / 4.5 cm to attach the ball to the star. With Skyline, crochet a chain of 1 in / 2.5 cm to attach the star to the Skyline pompom. Insert the wooden dowel in the twill loops. Place a ferrule at each end of the dowel.

Cut a length of White Phil Thalassa, about 21¾ in / 55 cm, and attach it to each end of the dowel.

14, 15 & 16
Lotus Undershirt and Pants, Sky Blue Undershirt

Baby's first outfit, made in stockinette stitch with garter stitch and ribbing details. Phil Coton 3 yarn. U.S. size 1-2 and 2-3 / 2.5 and 3 mm needles.

17 & 18
Pearl Undershirt and Pants

Good for girls as well as boys, a sweet color for this outfit made in stockinette stitch and ribbing details. Phil Coton 3 yarn. U.S. size 1-2 and 2-3 / 2.5 and 3 mm needles.

14 - *Lotus Undershirt*

SIZES

Newborn (3, 6, 9) months

MATERIALS

Yarn: CYCA #1, Phildar Phil Coton 3 (100% Cotton, 132 yd/121 m / 50 g), 2 (3, 3, 3) balls Lotus
Needles: U.S. sizes 1-2 and 2-3 / 2.5 and 3 mm

GAUGE

26 sts and 35 rows on larger needles = 4 x 4 in / 10 x 10 cm. Adjust needle sizes if necessary to obtain gauge.

PATTERN STITCHES

-Garter st: Knit every row
-Stockinette st: Knit on RS, purl on WS

INSTRUCTIONS

Back: With smaller needles, cast on 60 (62, 66, 70) sts. Work in garter st for ³⁄₈ in / 1 cm. Change to larger needles and work in St st.

When piece measures 3½ (4¼, 5¼, 5½) in / 9 (11, 13, 14) cm after the garter st, shape the armholes, at each side, on every other row: BO 3 sts once, 2 sts once, and 1 st 2 times (3 sts once, 2 sts once and 1 st once; 3 sts once, 2 sts once and 1 st once; 3 sts once, 2 sts once and 1 st 2 times) = 46 (50, 54, 56) sts. When piece measures 7½ (8¾, 9¾, 10¼) in / 19 (22, 25, 26) cm after the garter st, pm at edge sts and then, at each side, on every other row, inc 1 st 4 times.

At the same time, shape the neck: BO 10 (12, 14, 14) sts at center then work each side separately. On every other row, at neck edge, BO 5 sts once and 1 st 3 times.

When piece measures 8¾ (9¾, 11, 11½) in / 22 (25, 28, 29) cm after the garter st, BO rem 14 (15, 16, 17) sts. Work the other side of the neck the same way, reversing shaping.

Front: With smaller needles, cast on 60 (62, 66, 70) sts. Work in garter st for ³⁄₈ in / 1 cm. Change to larger needles and work in St st.

When piece measures 3½ (4¼, 5¼, 5½) in / (9 (11, 13, 14) cm after the garter st, shape the armholes, at each side, on every other row: BO 3 sts once, 2 sts once, and 1 st 2 times (3 sts once, 2 sts once and 1 st once; 3 sts once, 2 sts once and 1 st once; 3 sts once, 2 sts once and 1 st 2 times) = 46 (50, 54, 56) sts. When piece measures 6, (7, 8¼, 8¾) in / 15 (18, 21, 22) cm after garter st, shape neck: BO 8 (10, 12, 12) sts at center then work each side separately. On every other row, at neck edge, BO 2 sts 2 times and 1 st 2 times.

When piece measures 7 (8¼, 9½, 9¾) in / 18 (21, 24, 25) cm after garter st, shape the shoulders: on every other row at armhole edge, BO 4 sts 2 times and 5 sts once (4 sts once and 5 sts 2 times; 5 sts 3 times; 5 sts 2 times and 6 sts once). Work the other side of the neck the same way, reversing shaping.

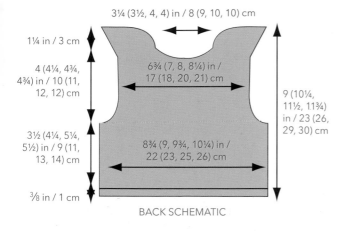

3¼ (3½, 4, 4) in / 8 (9, 10, 10) cm

1¼ in / 3 cm

4 (4¼, 4¾, 4¾) in / 10 (11, 12, 12) cm

6¾ (7, 8, 8¼) in / 17 (18, 20, 21) cm

9 (10¼, 11½, 11¾) in / 23 (26, 29, 30) cm

3½ (4¼, 5¼, 5½) in / 9 (11, 13, 14) cm

8¾ (9, 9¾, 10¼) in / 22 (23, 25, 26) cm

⅜ in / 1 cm

BACK SCHEMATIC

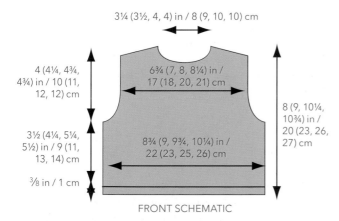

3¼ (3½, 4, 4) in / 8 (9, 10, 10) cm

4 (4¼, 4¾, 4¾) in / 10 (11, 12, 12) cm

6¾ (7, 8, 8¼) in / 17 (18, 20, 21) cm

8 (9, 10¼, 10¾) in / 20 (23, 26, 27) cm

3½ (4¼, 5¼, 5½) in / 9 (11, 13, 14) cm

8¾ (9, 9¾, 10¼) in / 22 (23, 25, 26) cm

⅜ in / 1 cm

FRONT SCHEMATIC

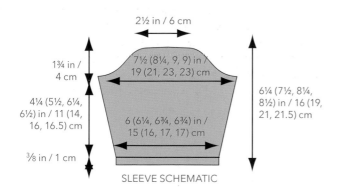

2½ in / 6 cm

1¾ in / 4 cm

7½ (8¼, 9, 9) in / 19 (21, 23, 23) cm

6¼ (7½, 8¼, 8½) in / 16 (19, 21, 21.5) cm

4¼ (5½, 6¼, 6½) in / 11 (14, 16, 16.5) cm

6 (6¼, 6¾, 6¾) in / 15 (16, 17, 17) cm

⅜ in / 1 cm

SLEEVE SCHEMATIC

Sleeves: With smaller needles, CO 42 (44, 46, 46) sts and work in garter st for ⅜ in / 1 cm. Change to larger needles. Continue in St st, increasing at each side as follows: on Row 8, inc 1 st and every 6th row inc 1 st 4 times (every 8th row inc 1 st 4 times and every 6th row inc 1 st 2 times; on Row 8, inc 1 st and every 6th row inc 1 st 7 times; every 8th row inc 1 st 2 times and every 6th row inc 1 st 6 times) = 52 (56, 62, 62) sts.

When piece measures 4¼ (5½, 6¼, 6½) in / 11 (14, 16, 16.5) cm after garter st, shape sleeve cap at the beg of each row as follows: every other row, BO 3 sts 2 times, 2 sts once, 1 st once, 2 sts once and 3 sts 2 times (3 sts 3 times, 2 sts 2 times and 3 sts 2 times; 4 sts once, 3 sts 2 times, 2 sts once, 3 sts 2 times and 4 sts once; 4 sts once, 3 sts 2 times, 2 sts once, 3 sts 2 times and 4 sts once).

When piece measures 6¼ (7½, 8¼, 8½) in / 16 (19, 21, 21.5) cm after garter st, loosely BO the rem 18 sts.

Pocket: With smaller needles, CO 26 (28, 31, 31) sts and work in garter st for ⅜ in / 1 cm. Change to larger needles and continue in St st.

When piece measures 1¾ (1¾, 2, 2) in / 4 (4.5, 5, 5) cm after garter st, BO loosely.

FINISHING

With smaller needles, pick up and knit 61 (66, 71, 71) sts around the neck and shoulders of the back. Work in garter st for ⅜ in / 1 cm then BO.

With smaller needles, pick up and knit 55 (60, 65, 65) sts around the neck and shoulders of the front. Work in garter st for ⅜ in / 1 cm then BO.

Sew the side and sleeve seams.

Fold the flaps of the back shoulders to the front and sew in place.

Sew the sleeves into the armholes and sew the pocket on the front.

15 - *Lotus Pants*

SIZES

Newborn (3, 6 to 9 months)

MATERIALS

Yarn: CYCA #1, Phildar Phil Coton 3 (100% Cotton, 132 yd/121 m / 50 g), 2 (2, 2) balls Lotus

Needles: U.S. sizes 1-2 and 2-3 / 2.5 and 3 mm

Notions: Elastic thread for the waist, 3 snaps, 3 buttons

GAUGE

26 sts and 35 rows on larger needles = 4 x 4 in / 10 x 10 cm. Adjust needle sizes if necessary to obtain gauge.

PATTERN STITCHES

-Ribbing: K1, p1

-Garter st: Knit every row

-Stockinette st: Knit on RS, purl on WS

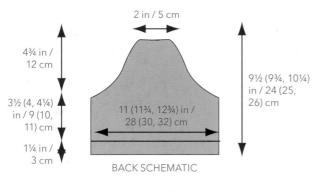

BACK SCHEMATIC

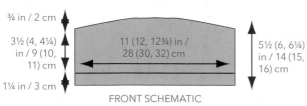

FRONT SCHEMATIC

INSTRUCTIONS

Back: With smaller needles, CO 72 (78, 84) sts and work in k1, p1 ribbing for 1¼ in / 3 cm. Change to larger needles and continue in St st.

When piece measures 3½ (4, 4¼) in / 9 (10, 11) cm after the ribbing, pm at edge sts and then shape curve at each side: on every other row, BO 2 sts 8 times and 1 st 13 times (2 sts 11 times and 1 st 10 times; 2 sts 14 times and 1 st 7 times).

When piece measures 8¼ (8¾, 9) in / 21 (22, 23) cm after ribbing, BO rem 14 sts.

Front: With smaller needles, CO 72 (78, 84) sts and work in k1, p1 ribbing for 1¼ in / 3 cm. Change to larger needles and continue in St st.

When piece measures 3½ (4, 4½) in / 9 (10, 11) cm after the ribbing, pm at edge sts and then shape each side as follows: on every other row, BO 11 sts once, 10 sts once, and 8 sts once (12 sts once, 11 sts once and 9 sts once; 13 sts once, 12 sts once and 10 sts once).

When piece measures 4¼ (4¾, 5¼) in / 11 (12, 13) cm after ribbing, BO rem 14 sts.

FINISHING

With smaller needles, pick up and knit 96 (102, 108) sts around the back curve (between the markers). Work in garter st for ⅜ in / 1 cm, then BO loosely.

With smaller needles, pick up and knit 72 (78, 84) sts in the BO row of the front. Work in garter st for ⅜ in / 1 cm, then BO loosely. Seam sides.

Sew on the snaps and then sew on a button over each snap.

Thread elastic through several rows of sts at the waist.

16 - *Sky Blue Undershirt*

SIZES
Newborn (3, 6, 9) months

MATERIALS
Yarn: CYCA #1, Phildar Phil Coton 3 (100% Cotton, 132 yd/121 m / 50 g), 3 (3, 3, 4) balls Sky blue; scrap yarn in a contrasting color (used for bands)
Needles: U.S. sizes 1-2 and 2-3 / 2.5 and 3 mm
Notions: 6 buttons and 3 snaps

GAUGE
26 sts and 35 rows in stockinette st on larger needles = 4 x 4 in / 10 x 10 cm. Adjust needle sizes if necessary to obtain gauge.

PATTERN STITCHES
-Ribbing: K3, p3
-Stockinette st: Knit on RS, purl on WS

INSTRUCTIONS
Back: With smaller needles, cast on 63 (63, 69, 69) sts. Work in k3, p3 ribbing for ¾ in / 2 cm, beginning and ending the first and all odd-numbered rows (RS) with k3.
With larger needles, continue in St st and dec 1 (inc 1, inc 1, inc 3 evenly spaced) on the first row = 62 (64, 70, 72) sts.

When piece measures 3¼ (4¼, 5, 5¼) in / 8.5 (10.5, 12.5, 13.5) cm after the ribbing, shape the raglan: at each side, BO 2 sts once, and then, on every other row:
Newborn: BO *1 st once, 2 sts once*; rep from * to * 6 more times and end by decreasing 1 st 3 times.
3 months: BO *1 st 2 times, 2 sts once; *rep from * to * 4 more times and end by decreasing 1 st 4 times.
6 months: BO *1 st 3 times, 2 sts once*; rep from * to * 4 more times and end by decreasing 1 st once.
9 months: BO *1 st 2 times, 2 sts once*; rep from * to * 5 more times and end by decreasing 1 st 3 times
When piece measures 7½ (8¾, 9¾, 10¼) in / 19 (22, 25, 26) cm after the ribbing, loosely BO 10 (12, 14, 14) rem sts.

Front: With smaller needles, CO 57 (57, 63, 63) sts and work in k3, p3 ribbing for ¾ in / 2 cm, beg the first and all odd-numbered rows (RS) with k4 and ending with k2.
With larger needles, continue in St st and dec 1 (inc 1, inc 1, inc 3 evenly spaced) on the first row = 56 (58, 64, 66) sts.
When piece measures 3¼ (4¼, 5, 5¼) in / 8.5 (10.5, 12.5, 13.5) cm after the ribbing, shape the raglan: at each side BO 2 sts once, and then, on every other row:
Newborn: BO *1 st once, 2 sts once*; rep from * to * 5 more times = 16 sts rem.
3 months: BO *1 st 2 times, 2 sts once*; rep from * to * 3 more times and end with dec 1 st 2 times = 18 sts rem.
6 months: BO *1 st 3 times, 2 sts once*; rep from * to * 3 more times = 20 sts rem.
9 months: BO *1 st 2 times, 2 sts once*; rep from * to * 4 more times and end with dec 1 st once = 20 sts rem.
The following instructions are for the right half of the front. Work each side separately and reverse the shaping for the left half. When piece measures 6¼ (7½, 8¾, 9) in / 16 (19, 22, 23) cm after the ribbing, shape the neck: at neck edge, BO 10 sts once, 1 st once, and 2 sts once (11 sts once and 2 sts

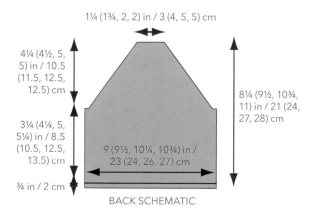

1¼ (1¾, 2, 2) in / 3 (4, 5, 5) cm

4¼ (4½, 5, 5) in / 10.5 (11.5, 12.5, 12.5) cm

8¼ (9½, 10¾, 11) in / 21 (24, 27, 28) cm

3¼ (4¼, 5, 5¼) in / 8.5 (10.5, 12.5, 13.5) cm

9 (9½, 10¼, 10¾) in / 23 (24, 26, 27) cm

¾ in / 2 cm

BACK SCHEMATIC

Sky Blue Undershirt (cont.)

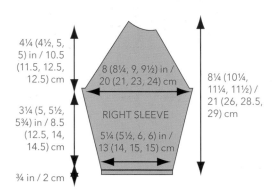

4¼ (4½, 5, 5) in / 10.5 (11.5, 12.5, 12.5) cm

8 (8¼, 9, 9½) in / 20 (21, 23, 24) cm

RIGHT SLEEVE

3¼ (5, 5½, 5¾) in / 8.5 (12.5, 14, 14.5) cm

5¼ (5½, 6, 6) in / 13 (14, 15, 15) cm

8¼ (10¼, 11¼, 11½) / 21 (26, 28.5, 29) cm

¾ in / 2 cm

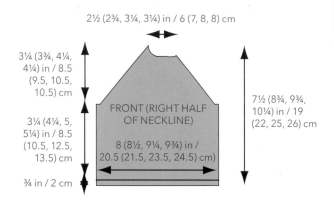

2½ (2¾, 3¼, 3¼) in / 6 (7, 8, 8) cm

3¼ (3¾, 4¼, 4¼) in / 8.5 (9.5, 10.5, 10.5) cm

FRONT (RIGHT HALF OF NECKLINE)

3¼ (4¼, 5, 5¼) in / 8.5 (10.5, 12.5, 13.5) cm

8 (8½, 9¼, 9¾) in / 20.5 (21.5, 23.5, 24.5) cm)

7½ (8¾, 9¾, 10¼) in / 19 (22, 25, 26) cm

¾ in / 2 cm

2 times; 13 sts once, 3 sts once and 2 sts once; 12 sts once, 3 sts once and 2 sts once). *At the same time*, at armhole edge, on every other row: BO 1 st once and 2 sts once (2 sts once and 1 st once; 1 st 2 times; 1 st once and 2 sts once).

Right Sleeve: With smaller needles, CO 38 sts for all sizes. Work in k3, p3 ribbing for ¾ in / 2 cm, beg the first and all odd-numbered rows (RS) with k3 and ending with k2.

With larger needles, continue in St st and on the first row dec 2 (dec 0, inc 2, inc 2) evenly spaced across = 36 (38, 40, 40) sts.

Inc at each side as follows: on every 4th row, inc 1 st 5 times and then, on every other row, inc 1 st 4 times (every 4th row, inc 1 st 9 times; work 5 rows then inc 1 st once and every 4th row, inc 1 st 10 times; inc 1 st every 4th row 12 times) = 54 (56, 62, 64) sts.

When piece measures 3¼ (5, 5½, 5¾) in / 8.5 (12.5, 14, 14.5) cm after the ribbing, shape the raglan: at the beg of each side, BO 2 sts once, and then, on every other row:

Newborn: BO *1 st once, 2 sts once*; rep from * to * 6 more times = 8 sts rem.

3 months: BO *1 st 2 times, 2 sts once*; rep from * to * 4 more times ending with 1 st once = 10 sts rem.

6 months: BO *1 st 3 times, 2 sts once*; rep from * to * 3 more times ending with 1 st 2 times = 14 sts rem.

9 months: BO *1 st 2 times, 2 sts once*; rep from * to * 5 more times = 12 sts rem.

When piece measures 6¾ (8¾, 9¾, 9¾) in / 17 (22, 24.5, 25) cm after the ribbing, on every other row at the right: BO 1 st 3 times and 2 sts once (3 sts once, 1 st 2 times and 2 sts once; 3 sts 2 times and 2 sts 2 times; 3 sts once and 2 sts 3 times).

At the same time, BO 1 st at the left side, then, on every other row: BO 1 st 2 times (1 st 2 times; 2 sts once and 1 st once; one st 2 times). Make the left sleeve the same way, reversing all shaping.

Button Bands: With smaller needles, CO 53 (59, 71, 71) sts and work in k3, p3 ribbing, beg and ending the first and all odd-numbered rows (RS) with k4. On the 3rd row, make 2 one-st buttonholes, the first 25 (26, 30, 32) sts from the left edge and the second spaced 14 (19, 27, 25) sts from the first.

When piece measures ¾ in / 2 cm, knit one row on the RS, then work a few rows of St st with scrap yarn. Ironing these rows will help in removing them for sewing.

Make a second band without buttonholes.

Neckband: With smaller needles, CO 71 (77, 89, 89) sts and work in k3, p3 ribbing, beg and ending the first and all the odd-numbered rows (RS) with k4. On the 3rd row, make a 1-st buttonhole 1 to 3 sts from the left edge.

When piece measures ¾ in / 2 cm, knit one row on the RS, then work a few rows of St st with scrap yarn. Ironing these rows will help in removing them for sewing.

FINISHING

Sew the sleeves to the body along the raglan (the smaller side is at the front).

Sew the side and sleeve seams.

RS facing, with back stitch, attach the button bands along the front st by st.

RS facing, with back stitch, attach the neckline band st by st.

Sew the snaps to the inside and sew a button over each snap.

Sew the buttons on the diagonal of the left front and on the neckline.

17 - *Pearl Sweater*

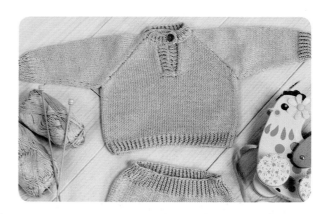

SIZES

Newborn (3, 6, 9) months

MATERIALS

Yarn: CYCA #1, Phildar Phil Coton 3 (100% Cotton, 132 yd/121 m / 50 g), 2 (2, 3, 3) balls Pearl; scrap yarn in a contrasting color (used for bands)

Needles: U.S. sizes 1-2 and 2-3 / 2.5 and 3 mm

Notions: 1 button

GAUGE

26 sts and 35 rows in stockinette st on larger needles = 4 x 4 in / 10 x 10 cm in. Adjust needle sizes if necessary to obtain gauge.

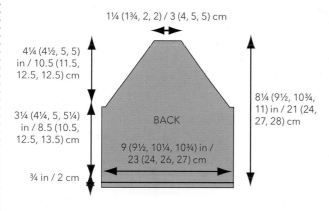

1¼ (1¾, 2, 2) / 3 (4, 5, 5) cm

4¼ (4½, 5, 5) in / 10.5 (11.5, 12.5, 12.5) cm

3¼ (4¼, 5, 5¼) in / 8.5 (10.5, 12.5, 13.5) cm

BACK

8¼ (9½, 10¾, 11) in / 21 (24, 27, 28) cm

9 (9½, 10¼, 10¾) in / 23 (24, 26, 27) cm

¾ in / 2 cm

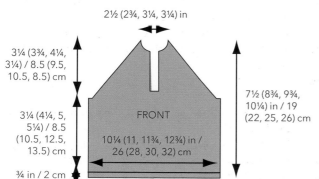

2½ (2¾, 3¼, 3¼) in

3¼ (3¾, 4¼, 3¼) / 8.5 (9.5, 10.5, 8.5) cm

3¼ (4¼, 5, 5¼) / 8.5 (10.5, 12.5, 13.5) cm

FRONT

7½ (8¾, 9¾, 10¼) in / 19 (22, 25, 26) cm

10¼ (11, 11¾, 12¾) in / 26 (28, 30, 32) cm

¾ in / 2 cm

PATTERN STITCHES

-Ribbing: K1, p1

-Stockinette st: Knit on RS, purl on WS

INSTRUCTIONS

Back: With smaller needles, CO 62 (64, 70, 72) sts and work in k1, p1 ribbing for ¾ in / 2 cm. Change to larger needles and continue in St st.

When piece measures 3¼ (4¼, 5, 5¼) in / 8.5 (10.5, 12.5, 13.5) cm after the ribbing, shape the raglan: at each side, BO 2 sts once, and then, on every other row:

Newborn: BO *1 st once, 2 sts once*; rep from * to * 6 more times, then 1 st 3 times.

3 months: BO *1 st 2 times, 2 sts once*; rep from * to * 4 more times, then 1 st 4 times.

6 months: BO *1 st 3 times, 2 sts once*; rep from * to * 4 more times, then 1 st once.

9 months: BO *1 st 2 times, 2 sts once*; rep from * to * 5 more times, then 1 st 3 times.

When piece measures 7½ (8¾, 9¾, 10¼) in / 19 (22, 25, 26) cm after the ribbing, loosely bind off the rem 10 (12, 14, 14) sts.

Front: With smaller needles, CO 62 (64, 70, 72) sts and work in k1, p1 ribbing for ¾ in / 2 cm. Change to larger needles and continue in St st.

When piece measures 3¼ (4¼, 5, 5¼) in / 8.5 (10.5, 12.5, 13.5) cm after the ribbing, shape the raglan: at each side, BO 2 sts once, and then, every other row:

Newborn: BO *1 st once, 2 sts once*; rep from * to * 6 more times = 16 sts rem.

3 months: BO *1 st 2 times, 2 sts once*; rep from * to * 4 more times, then 1 st once =18 sts rem.

6 months: BO *1 st 3 times, 2 sts once*; rep from * to * 3 more times, then 1 st 2 times = 22 sts rem.

9 months: BO *1 st 2 times, 2 sts once*; rep from * to * 5 more times = 20 sts rem.

Pearl Sweater (cont.)

When piece measures 3¼ (4¼, 5½, 6) in / 8 (11, 14, 15) cm after the ribbing, make an opening by binding off the center 4 sts. Work each side separately. When piece measures 6 (7, 8¼, 8¾) in / 15 (18, 21, 22) cm after the ribbing, at the neck opening, on every other row BO 2 sts 3 times (3 sts once and 2 sts 2 times; 4 sts once, 3 sts once, and 2 sts once; 3 sts 2 times and 2 sts once). Work the opposite side the same way, reversing shaping.

Right Sleeve: With smaller needles, CO 36 (38, 40, 40) sts and work in k1, p1 ribbing for ¾ in / 2 cm. With larger needles, continue in St st, increasing at each side as follows: on every 4th row, inc 1 st 5 times and on every other row, inc 1 st 4 times (every 4th row, 1 st 9 times; after 6 rows, 1 st once and every 4th row, 1 st 10 times; every 4th row, 1 st 12 times) = 54 (56, 62, 64) sts.
When piece measures 3¼ (5, 5½, 5¾) in / 8.5 (12.5, 14, 14.5) cm after the ribbing, shape the raglan: at each side, BO 2 sts once, and then, on every other row:

Newborn: BO *1 st once, 2 sts once*; rep from * to * 6 more times = 8 sts rem.
3 months: BO *1 st 2 times, 2 sts once*; rep from * to * 4 more times ending with 1 st once = 10 sts rem.
6 months: BO *1 st 3 times, 2 sts once*; rep from * to * 3 more times ending with 1 st 2 times = 14 sts rem.
9 months: BO *1 st 2 times, 2 sts once*; rep from * to * 5 more times = 12 sts rem.

When piece measures 6¾ (8¾, 9¾, 9¾) in / 17 (22, 24.5, 25) cm after the ribbing, at the right on every other row: BO 1 st 3 times and 2 sts once (3 sts once, 1 st 2 times, and 2 sts once; 3 sts 2 times and 2 sts 2 times; 3 sts once and 2 sts 3 times).

At the same time, BO at the left 1 st once then every other row 1 st 2 times (1 st 2 times; 2 sts once and 1 st once; 1 st 2 times).
Make the left sleeve the same way, reversing all shaping.

Neck Placket Bands: With smaller needles, CO 19 sts and work in k1, p1 ribbing for ¾ in / 2 cm, beg and ending the first and all odd-numbered rows (RS) with k2. Knit 1 row on RS, then work a few rows in St st with scrap yarn. Ironing these rows will help in removing them for sewing.

Neckband: With smaller needles, CO 56 (59, 61, 61) sts and work in k1, p1 ribbing, beg and ending the first and all odd-numbered rows (RS) with k2.
Make a one-st buttonhole on the 3rd row 3 sts from the left edge.
When piece measures ¾ in / 2 cm, k51 (54, 56, 56) on the RS and BO the last 5 sts.
With scrap yarn, work a few rows of St st on the rem 51 (54, 56, 56) sts.
Ironing these rows will help in removing them for sewing.

FINISHING

Sew the sleeves to the body along the raglan shaping, the smaller side at the front.
Sew the side and sleeve seams.
With RS facing, back stitch the placket bands to the front opening, st by st, and sew on neckband the same way. Sew on the button.

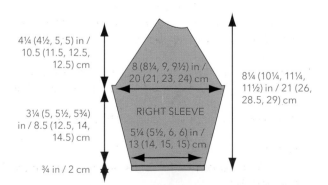

4¼ (4½, 5, 5) in / 10.5 (11.5, 12.5, 12.5) cm

3¼ (5, 5½, 5¾) in / 8.5 (12.5, 14, 14.5) cm

¾ in / 2 cm

8 (8¼, 9, 9½) in / 20 (21, 23, 24) cm

RIGHT SLEEVE

5¼ (5½, 6, 6) in / 13 (14, 15, 15) cm

8¼ (10¼, 11¼, 11½) in / 21 (26, 28.5, 29) cm

18 - *Pants*

SIZES

Newborn (3, 6-9) months

MATERIALS

Yarn: CYCA #1, Phildar Phil Coton 3 (100% Cotton, 132 yd/121 m / 50 g), 2 (2, 2) balls Pearl; scrap yarn in a contrasting color (used for bands)
Needles: U.S. sizes 1-2 and 2-3 / 2.5 and 3 mm
Notions: Elastic thread; stitch holder

GAUGE

With larger needles, 26 sts and 35 rows = 4 x 4 in / 10 x 10 cm in stockinette stitch. Adjust needle size if necessary to obtain gauge.

PATTERN STITCHES

-Ribbing: K1, p1
-Stockinette st: Knit on RS, purl on WS

INSTRUCTIONS

Back: With smaller needles, CO 28 (29, 32) sts for the back of one leg. Work in k1, p1 ribbing for ¾ in / 2 cm. With larger needles, continue in St st. When piece measures 1½ (1¾, 2) in / 3.5 (4, 5) cm after the ribbing, inc 1 st at the right side. After 2 rows, inc 2 sts at right side = 31 (32, 35) sts. When piece measures 1¾ (2, 2½) in / 4.5 (5, 6) cm after the ribbing, slip the sts to a

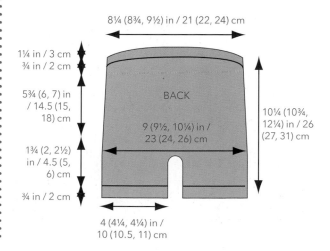

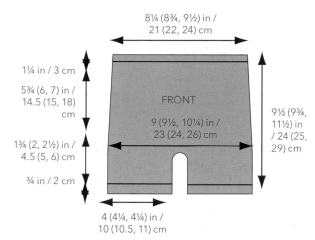

holder and make the second back of leg, reversing the shaping. Join the 2 half-legs, increasing one st at the center = 63 (65, 71) sts.

Continue in St st, decreasing at each side as follows: 1 st on row 18 and 1 st 16 rows later (one st every 18th row 2 times, 1 st every 22nd row 2 times) = 59 (61, 67) sts.

When piece measures 7½ (8, 9½) in / 19 (20, 24) cm after the ribbing, work short rows (see Short Rows in Basic Information, page 160), leaving sts unworked at each side on every other row as follows: 4 sts once and 5 sts 2 times (5 sts 3 times, 6 sts 3 times). When piece measures 8¼ (8¾, 10¼) in / 21 (22, 26) cm after the ribbing at the bottom of the legs, switch back to smaller needles and work in k1, p1 ribbing for 1¼ in / 3 cm. BO all sts loosely.

Front: With smaller needles, CO 28 (29, 32) sts for the front of one leg. Work in k1, p1 ribbing for ¾ in / 2 cm. With larger needles, continue in St st. When piece measures 1½ (1¾, 2) in / 3.5 (4, 5) cm after the ribbing, inc 1 st at the right side. Work 2 more rows and then inc 2 sts at right side = 31 (32, 35) sts.

When piece measures 1¾ (2, 2½) in / 4.5 (5, 6) cm after the ribbing, sl sts to a holder and make the second front of leg, reversing the shaping. Join the 2 half-legs, increasing one st in the center = 63 (65, 71) sts.

Continue in St st, decreasing at each side as follows: 1 st after 18 rows and 1 st after 16 rows (one st every 18th row 2 times, 1 st every 22nd row 2 times) = 59 (61, 67) sts.

When piece measures 7½ (8, 9½) in / 19 (20, 24) cm after the ribbing at the bottom of legs, switch back to smaller needles and continue in k1, p1 ribbing.

When piece measures 8¾ (9, 10¾) in / 22 (23, 27) cm, loosely BO all sts.

FINISHING

Sew the side and crotch seams. Thread several rows of elastic through waistband stitches.

19 - *Dress*

An adorable dress tied at the waist, in stockinette st with garter st details. Phildar Muse and Phildar Phil Ecolo yarns. U.S. sizes 4 and 6 / 3.5 and 4 mm needles.

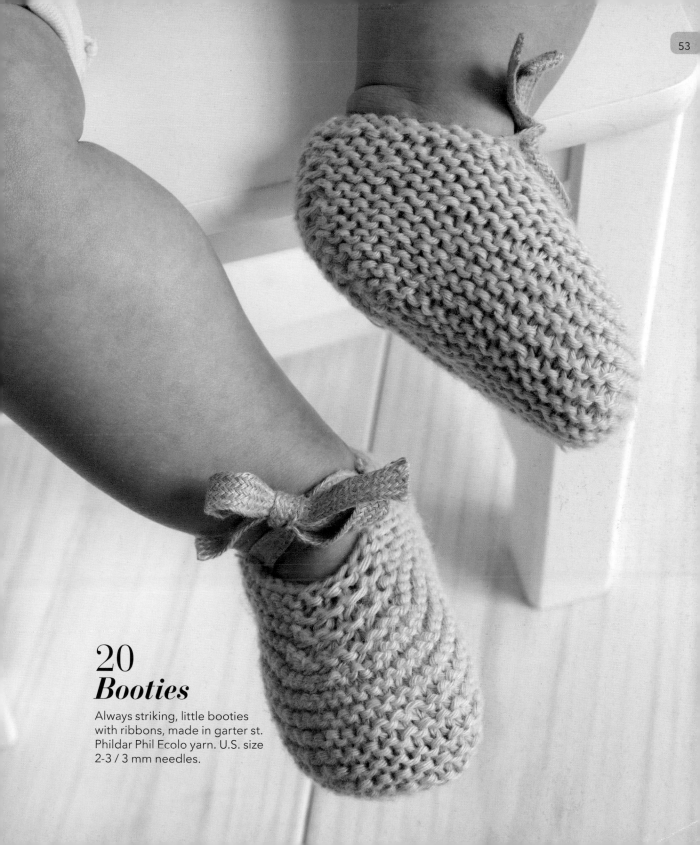

20
Booties

Always striking, little booties
with ribbons, made in garter st.
Phildar Phil Ecolo yarn. U.S. size
2-3 / 3 mm needles.

19 - *Dress*

SIZES

Newborn (3, 6, 9) months

MATERIALS

Yarn: CYCA #2, Phildar Muse (50% Cotton, 28% Linen, 22% Tencel; 121 yds/ 111 m / 50 g), 3 (3, 4, 4) balls Nutmeg and CYCA #3, Phildar Phil Ecolo (100% Polyester, 105 yds/96 m / 50 g), 1 ball Sherbet; scrap yarn in a contrasting color (used for bands)

Needles: U.S. sizes 4 and 6 / 3.5 and 4 mm

Notions: 21¼ in / 54 cm beige cotton ribbon

GAUGE

21 sts and 27 rows in St st on larger needles = 4 x 4 in / 10 x 10 cm. Adjust needle sizes if necessary to obtain gauge.

PATTERN STITCHES

-Garter st: Knit every row

-Stockinette st: Knit on RS, purl on WS

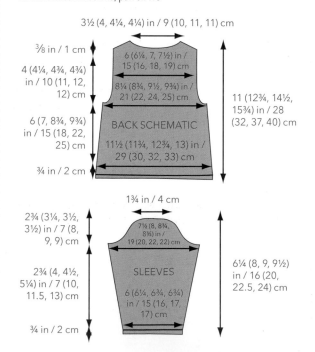

3½ (4, 4¼, 4¼) in / 9 (10, 11, 11) cm

⅜ in / 1 cm

4 (4¼, 4¾, 4¾) in / 10 (11, 12, 12) cm

6 (6¼, 7, 7½) in / 15 (16, 18, 19) cm

8¼ (8¾, 9½, 9¾) in / 21 (22, 24, 25) cm

11 (12¾, 14½, 15¾) in / 28 (32, 37, 40) cm

BACK SCHEMATIC

6 (7, 8¾, 9¾) in / 15 (18, 22, 25) cm

11½ (11¾, 12¾, 13) in / 29 (30, 32, 33) cm

¾ in / 2 cm

1¾ in / 4 cm

2¾ (3¼, 3½, 3½) in / 7 (8, 9, 9) cm

7½ (8, 8¾, 8¾) in / 19 (20, 22, 22) cm

SLEEVES

6¼ (8, 9, 9½) in / 16 (20, 22.5, 24) cm

2¾ (4, 4½, 5¼) in / 7 (10, 11.5, 13) cm

6 (6¼, 6¾, 6¾) in / 15 (16, 17, 17) cm

¾ in / 2 cm

-Dec 1 st from the edges as follows: On the right: K1, k2tog and on the left: knit to the last 3 sts, ssk, k last st

INSTRUCTIONS

Back: With smaller needles and Sherbet, CO 62 (64, 70, 72) sts and work in garter st for ¾ in / 2 cm (6 rows = 3 ridges). With Nutmeg and larger needles, continue in St st, decreasing 1 st at each side (see Pattern Stitches) as follows: every 6th row 3 times and every 4th row 5 times (every 6th row 7 times and after 4 rows once; after 8 rows once and every 6th row 8 times; every 8th row 5 times and every 6th row 4 times) = 46 (48, 52, 54) sts.

When piece measures 6 (7, 8¾, 9¾) in / 15 (18, 22, 25) cm after garter st, shape the armholes: at each side, on every other row, BO 3 sts once, 2 sts once, and 1 st once = 34 (36, 40, 42) sts.

When piece measures 9¾, 11½, 13½, 14½) in / 25 (29, 34, 37) cm after garter st, shape the shoulders: at each side, on every other row, BO 4 sts 2 times (4 sts 2 times, 4 sts 2 times, 4 sts once and 5 sts once).

At the same time, shape the neck, binding off the 18 (20, 24, 24) center sts; work each side separately.

Front: Work as for the back to the armholes = 34 (36, 40, 42) sts.

When piece measures 7 (8¾, 10¾, 11¾) in / 18 (22, 27, 30) cm after garter st, make an opening by binding off the 4 center sts. Work each side separately.

When piece measures 8¼ (9¾, 11¾, 13) in / 21 (25, 30, 33) cm after garter st, shape the neckline: at neck edge on every other row, BO 2 sts 2 times, 1 st 2 times and, after 4 rows, 1 st (3 sts once, 2 sts once, 1 st 2 times and, after 4 rows, 1 st; 3 sts once, 2 sts 2 times and 1 st 3 times; 3 sts once, 2 sts 2 times, and 1 st 3 times).

When piece measures 9¾ (11½, 13½, 14½) in / 25 (29, 34, 37) cm after garter st, shape the shoulder: at armhole edge on every other row, BO 4 sts 2 times (4 sts 2 times, 4 sts 2 times, 4 sts once and 5 sts once).

Sleeves: With smaller needles and Sherbet, CO 34 (36, 38, 38) sts and work in garter st for ¾ in / 2 cm (6 rows = 3 ridges). With larger needles and Nutmeg, continue in St st, increasing at each side as follows: every 4th row 4 times (every 6th row 4 times, every 6th row 4 times and then once after 4 rows, every 6th row 5 times) = 42 (44, 48, 48) sts. When piece measures 2¾ (4, 4½, 5¼) in / 7 (10, 11.5, 13) cm after garter st, shape the sleeve cap: at each side, on every other row, BO 2 sts 3 times, 1 st 4 times, and 2 sts 3 times (2 sts 3 times, 1 st 5 times, and 2 sts 3 times; 2 sts 3 times, 1 st 7 times, and 2 sts 3 times; 2

sts 3 times, 1 st 7 times and 2 sts 3 times). When piece measures 5½ (7, 8, 8¾) in / 14 (18, 20.5, 22) cm after garter st, loosely BO the 10 rem sts.

Pocket: With smaller needles and Sherbet, CO 14 sts and work in garter st for ¾ in / 2 cm (6 rows = 3 ridges). Continue in St st for ¾ in / 2 cm, then, at each side on every other row, BO 1 st 3 times and 2 sts once. When piece measures 1¾ in / 4 cm after garter st, BO the 4 rem sts.

Detail Bands (make 2 alike): With smaller needles and Sherbet, CO 8 sts and work in garter st for ¾ in / 2 cm (6 rows = 3 ridges), and then work a few rows of St st with scrap yarn. Ironing these rows will help in removing them for sewing.

Neckband: With smaller needles and Sherbet, CO 56 (60, 64, 64) sts and work in garter st for ¾ in / 2 cm (6 rows = 3 ridges), and then work a few rows of St st with scrap yarn. Ironing these rows will help in removing them for sewing.

FINISHING

Sew the shoulder, side, and sleeve seams.
Sew the sleeves to the armholes. With RS facing, back stitch the detail bands along the front opening st by st and back stitch the neckline band in the same way. Sew the pocket on the front of the dress 2¼ (2¾, 3½, 4) in / 5.5 (7, 9, 10) cm from the bottom. Cut the ribbon in half and sew a length to each side of the front, under the armhole.

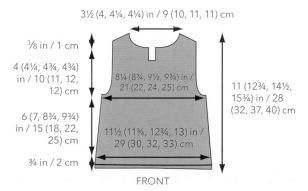

3½ (4, 4¼, 4¼) in / 9 (10, 11, 11) cm

⅜ in / 1 cm

4 (4¼, 4¾, 4¾) in / 10 (11, 12, 12) cm

8¼ (8¾, 9½, 9¾) in / 21 (22, 24, 25) cm

11 (12¾, 14½, 15¾) in / 28 (32, 37, 40) cm

6 (7, 8¾, 9¾) in / 15 (18, 22, 25) cm

11½ (11¾, 12¾, 13) in / 29 (30, 32, 33) cm

¾ in / 2 cm

FRONT

20 - *Booties*

SIZE
Newborn to 3 months

MATERIALS
Yarn: CYCA #3, Phildar Phil Ecolo (100% Polyester, 105 yds/96 m / 50 g), 1 ball Sherbet
Needles: U.S. sizes 2-3 / 3 mm
Notions: 21¼ in / 54 cm beige cotton ribbon to match the dress

PATTERN STITCHES
-Garter st: Knit every row
-M1 inc: Lift strand between 2 sts and knit into back loop

INSTRUCTIONS (MAKE 2 ALIKE)
CO 31 sts for the sole and work 2 rows of garter st, then continue as follows:
Row 3: K1, M1, k14, M1, k1, M1, k14, M1, k1.
Row 4 and all even-numbered rows: Knit.
Row 5: K2, M1, k14, M1, k3, M1, k14, M1 and k2.
Row 7: K3, M1, k14, M1, k5, M1, k14, M1, and k3.
Row 9: K4, M1, k14, M1, k7, M1, k14, M1, and k4.
Row 11: K5, M1, k14, M1, k9, M1, k14, M1, and k5 = 51 sts.
Rows 13 and 14: Knit. This completes the sole.
Continue in garter st for the foot. When piece measures 1¾ in / 4 cm, shape the top of the foot as follows: K16, (k2tog) 9 times, k17. Work one row without shaping and then k15, (k2tog) 6 times, k15. Work one row without shaping and then k13, (k2tog) 5 times, k13 = 31 sts. When piece measures 2½ in / 6 cm, loosely bind off all the sts.

FINISHING
Sew the heel and sole seams. Cut the ribbon into 4 equal lengths. Sew a ribbon at each side of the bootie 1 in / 2.5 cm from the heel seam.

21 - *Sleeveless Overalls*

Refined, sleeveless overalls. Knit in stockinette stitch and 2/2 ribbing. Phil Coton 3 yarn. U.S. size 1-2 and 2-3 / 2.5 and 3 mm needles.

22, 23 & 24
Short-sleeved Overalls and Socks

Overalls with sleeves and stripes. Matching socks. Knit in stockinette st and 2/2 ribbing. Phil Coton 3 yarn. U.S. size 1-2 and 2-3 / 2.5 and 3 mm needles.

21 - *Sleeveless Overalls*

SIZES

Newborn (3, 6, 9) months

MATERIALS

Yarn: CYCA #1, Phildar Phil Coton 3 (100% Cotton, 132 yd/121 m / 50 g), 2 (2, 3, 3) balls Mercury and 1 (1, 1, 2) balls Dew; scrap yarn in a contrasting color (used for bands)

Needles: U.S. sizes 1-2 and 2-3 / 2.5 and 3 mm

Notions: 9 buttons and 5 snaps; stitch holder

GAUGE

26 sts and 35 rows in St st on larger needles = 4 x 4 in / 10 x 10 cm. Adjust needle sizes if necessary to obtain gauge.

PATTERN STITCHES

-Ribbing: K2, p2
-Stockinette st: Knit on RS, purl on WS

INSTRUCTIONS

Back: Begin at back of one leg. With smaller needles and Dew, CO 30 (30, 34, 34) sts. Work in k2, p2 ribbing for ⅝ in / 1.5 cm, beg and ending the first and all odd-numbered rows (RS) with k2. With larger needles and Mercury, continue in St st, increasing 0 (1, 0, 0) sts on the first row = 30 (31, 34, 34) sts.

When piece measures 1½ (2, 2½, 2¾) in / 3.5 (5, 6, 7) cm after the ribbing, shape the crotch: at the right edge on every other row, inc 1 st 3 times and 2 sts once = 35 (36, 39, 39) sts.

When piece measures 2½ (3¼, 3½, 4) in / 6.5 (8, 9, 10) cm after the ribbing, sl sts to a holder. Work the back of the other leg, reversing the shaping.

Working on all 70 (72, 78, 78) sts, dec at each side as follows: 1 st every 12th row 5 times (1 st every 14th row 2 times and 1 st every 12th row 3 times; 1 st on the 14th row and then 1 st 5 times every 12th row; 1 st every 20th row 3 times and then 1 st after 18 rows) = 60 (62, 66, 70) sts.

When piece measures 10½ (11¾, 13¼, 14¾) in / 26.5 (29.5, 33.5, 37.5) cm after the ribbing, shape the armholes: at each side on every other row, BO 3 sts once, 2 sts 2 times, and 1 st once = 44 (46, 50, 54) sts.

When piece measures 14 (15½, 17½, 19) in / 35.5 (39.5, 44.5, 48.5) sts after the ribbing, shape the neck, binding off the 10 (12, 14, 14) center sts, and then continue each side separately. Work 2 rows and then BO 7 sts at neck edge. When piece measures 14½ (16, 18, 19½) in / 36.5 (40.5, 45.5, 49.5) cm after the ribbing, BO the 10 (10, 11, 13) rem sts for the shoulder.

Front: Begin at front of one leg. With smaller needles and Dew, CO 30 (30, 34, 34) sts. Work in k2, p2 ribbing for ⅝ in / 1.5 cm, beg and ending the first and all odd-numbered rows (RS) with k2. With larger needles and Mercury, continue in St st, increasing 0 (1, 0, 0) sts on the first row = 30 (31, 34, 34) sts.

When piece measures 1½ (2, 2½, 2¾) in / 3.5 (5, 6, 7) cm after the ribbing, shape the crotch: at the right edge on every other row, inc 1 st 3 times and 2 sts once = 35 (36, 39, 39) sts.

When piece measures 2½ (3¼, 3½, 4) in / 6.5 (8, 9, 10) cm after the ribbing, sl sts to a holder. Work the front of the other leg the same way, reversing the shaping.

Working on all 70 (72, 78, 78) sts, dec at each side as follows: 1 st every 12th row 5 times (1 st every 14th row 2 times and 1 st every 12th row 3 times; 1 st on the 14th row and then 1 st 5 times every 12th row; 1 st every 20th row 3 times and then 1 st after 18 rows).

At the same time, when piece measures 7 (7¾, 10½, 12) in / 17.5 (19.5, 26.5, 30.5) cm after the ribbing, work on the first 50 (51, 53, 54) sts and slip the sts at the left to a holder.

When piece measures 9 (9¾, 12½, 14) in / 22.5 (24.5, 31.5, 35.5) cm after the ribbing, shape the neckline: BO 2 sts once, then, on every other row, BO 2 sts 4 times and 1 st 20 times (2 sts 5 times and 1 st 19 times; 2 sts 6 times and 1 st 18 times; 2 sts 6 times and 1 st 18 times).

When piece measures 10½ (11¾, 13¼, 14¾) in / 26.5 (29.5, 33.5, 37.5) cm after the ribbing, shape the armholes: on every other row at the outside edge, BO 3 sts once, 2 sts 2 times, and 1 st once.

At the same time, when piece measures 14½ in / 36.5 cm after the ribbing, bind off 10 (10, 11, 13) sts for the shoulder. Continue working the 14 (15, 17, 18) sts from the holder and CO 36 additional sts at the left edge = 50 (51, 53, 54) sts. Work this side as for opposite side, reversing shaping.

Armhole Bands (make 2 alike): With smaller needles and Dew, CO 62 (66, 70, 70) sts and work in k2, p2 ribbing for ⅝ in / 1.5 cm, beg and ending the first and all odd-numbered rows (RS) with k2. Knit 1 row on the RS and then work a few additional rows of St st with scrap yarn. Ironing these rows will help in removing them for sewing.

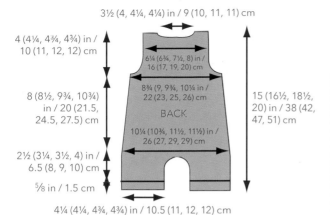

3½ (4, 4¼, 4¼) in / 9 (10, 11, 11) cm

4 (4¼, 4¾, 4¾) in / 10 (11, 12, 12) cm

6¼ (6¾, 7½, 8) in / 16 (17, 19, 20) cm

8¾ (9, 9¾, 10¼ / 22 (23, 25, 26) cm

BACK

10¼ (10¾, 11½, 11½) in / 26 (27, 29, 29) cm

8 (8½, 9¾, 10¾) in / 20 (21.5, 24.5, 27.5) cm

15 (16½, 18½, 20) in / 38 (42, 47, 51) cm

2½ (3¼, 3½, 4) in / 6.5 (8, 9, 10) cm

⅝ in / 1.5 cm

4¼ (4¼, 4¾, 4¾) in / 10.5 (11, 12, 12) cm

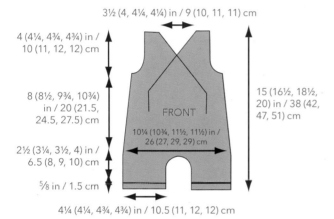

3½ (4, 4¼, 4¼) in / 9 (10, 11, 11) cm

4 (4¼, 4¾, 4¾) in / 10 (11, 12, 12) cm

FRONT

10¼ (10¾, 11½, 11½) in / 26 (27, 29, 29) cm

8 (8½, 9¾, 10¾) in / 20 (21.5, 24.5, 27.5) cm

15 (16½, 18½, 20) in / 38 (42, 47, 51) cm

2½ (3¼, 3½, 4) in / 6.5 (8, 9, 10) cm

⅝ in / 1.5 cm

4¼ (4¼, 4¾, 4¾) in / 10.5 (11, 12, 12) cm

Neckband: With smaller needles and Dew, CO 160 (164, 168, 168) sts and work in k2, p2 ribbing, beg and ending the first and all odd-numbered rows (RS) with k3. On the 3rd row, make 4 two-st buttonholes; the 1st should be 7 sts from the edge, the others 11 sts apart. When piece measures ⅝ in / 1.5 cm, knit 1 row on the RS, and then work a few additional rows of St st with scrap yarn. Ironing these rows will help in removing them for sewing.

Crotch Bands (make 2 alike): With smaller needles and Dew, CO 9 sts and work in k1, p1 ribbing for 7 (8¼, 9, 9¾) in / 18 (21, 23, 25) cm, beg and ending the first and all odd-numbered rows (RS) with k2. BO.

FINISHING

Sew the shoulder seams. With RS facing, backstitch the bands in the armholes, st by st. Sew the side seams. Sew on the crotch bands. With RS facing, backstitch the bands at the neck, st by st. Sew the snaps to the crotch bands, sew a button over each snap, and sew on the rem buttons. With 2 strands of Dew, make 2 twisted cords 6 in / 15 cm long when finished. Sew one to the tip of the front neckline (the underneath part) and one cord on the side seam.

22 - Short-sleeved Overalls

SIZES

Newborn (3, 6, 9) months

MATERIALS

Yarn: CYCA #1, Phildar Phil Coton 3 (100% Cotton, 132 yd/121 m / 50 g), 2 (2, 3, 3) balls Mercury and 2 (2, 2, 2) balls Sky Blue; scrap yarn in a contrasting color (used for bands)
Needles: U.S. sizes 1-2 and 2-3 / 2.5 and 3
Notions: 9 buttons and 5 snaps; stitch holder

GAUGE

26 sts and 35 rows in striped stockinette st on larger needles = 4 x 4 in / 10 x 10 cm. Adjust needle sizes if necessary to obtain gauge.

PATTERN STITCHES

-Ribbing: K2, p2
-Stockinette st: Striped in *2 rows Mercury and 2 rows Sky Blue*; rep from * to *

INSTRUCTIONS

Back: Beg with the back of one leg. With smaller needles and Mercury, CO 30 (30, 34, 34) sts. Work in k2, p2 ribbing for ⅝ in / 1.5 cm, beg and ending the first and all odd-numbered rows (RS) with k2. Change to larger needles and striped pattern in St st, increasing 0 (1, 0, 0) sts on the first row = 30 (31, 34, 34) sts.

When piece measures 1½ (2, 2½, 2¾) in / 3.5 (5, 6, 7) cm after the ribbing, shape the crotch: at the right edge, on every other row, inc 1 st 3 times and 2 sts once = 35 (36, 39, 39) sts.

When piece measures 2½ (3¼, 3½, 4) in / 6.5 (8, 9, 10) cm after the ribbing, sl sts to a holder. Work the back of the other leg the same way, reversing the shaping.

Working on all 70 (72, 78, 78) sts, dec at each side as follows: 1 st every 12th row 5 times (1 st every 14th row 2 times and 1 st every 12th row 3 times; 1 st on the 14th row, and then 1 st 5 times every 12th row; 1 st every 20th row 3 times and then 1 st after 18 rows) = 60 (62, 66, 70) sts.

When piece measures 10½ (11¾, 13¼, 14¾) in / 26.5 (29.5, 33.5, 37.5) cm after the ribbing, shape the armholes: at each side on every other row, BO 3 sts once, 2 sts 2 times, and 1 st once = 44 (46, 50, 54) sts.

Overalls (cont.)

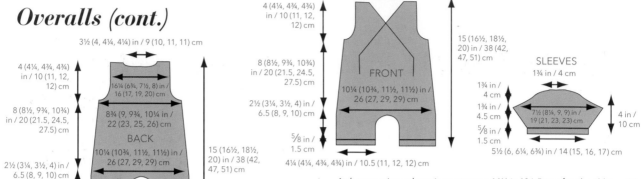

At the same time, when piece measures 14½ in / 36.5 cm after the ribbing, BO 10 (10, 11, 13) sts for the shoulder. Continue working the 14 (15, 17, 18) sts from the holder and CO 36 additional sts at the left edge = 50 (51, 53, 54) sts. Finish this side as for opposite side, reversing the shaping.

Sleeves: With smaller needles and Mercury, CO 38 (42, 42, 46) sts. Work in k2, p2 ribbing for ⅝ in / 1.5 cm, beg and ending the first row and all odd-numbered rows (RS) with k2. Change to larger needles and striped pattern in St st, increasing 0 (0, 2, 0) on the first row = 38 (42, 44, 46) sts. Inc 1 st at each side every other row 7 times = 52 (56, 58, 60) sts.

When piece measures 1¾ in / 4.5 cm after the ribbing, shape the sleeve cap, binding off at each side every other row as follows: 4 sts once, 3 sts once, 2 sts 3 times, 3 sts once and 4 sts once (4 sts once, 3 sts 2 times, 2 sts once, 3 sts 2 times, and 4 sts once; 4 sts once, 3 sts 5 times, and 4 sts once; 5 sts once, 4 sts once, 3 sts once, 2 sts once, 3 sts 2 times, and 4 sts once). When piece measures 3¼ in / 8.5 cm after the ribbing, BO 12 rem sts.

Neckband: With smaller needles and Mercury, CO 160 (164, 168, 168) sts and work in k2, p2 ribbing, beg and ending the first and all odd-numbered rows (RS) with k3. On Row 3, make 4 two-st buttonholes, the first 7 sts from the edge and the others 11 sts apart. When piece measures ⅝ in / 1.5 cm, knit 1 row on the RS, and then a few additional rows of St st with scrap yarn. Ironing these rows will help in removing them for sewing.

Crotch Bands (make 2 alike): With smaller needles and Dew, CO 9 sts and work in k1, p1 ribbing for 7 (8¼, 9, 9¾) in / 18 (21, 23, 25) cm, beg and ending the first and all odd-numbered rows (RS) with k2. BO.

FINISHING

Sew the shoulder, side, and sleeve seams. Sew sleeves to the armholes. Sew on the crotch bands. With RS facing, backstitch the bands to the neck, st by st. Sew the snaps to the crotch bands, sew a button over each snap, and sew on the rem buttons. Using 2 strands of Mercury, make 2 twisted cords about 6 in / 15 cm long when finished. Sew one to the tip of the front neckline (the underneath part) and one cord on the side seam.

When piece measures 14 (15½, 17½, 19) in / 35.5 (39.5, 44.5, 48.5) cm after the ribbing, shape the neck: BO the 10 (12, 14, 14) center sts, then continue each side separately. Work 2 rows and then BO 7 sts at neck edge.

When piece measures 14½ (16, 18, 19½) in / 36.5 (40.5, 45.5, 49.5) cm after the ribbing, BO the 10 (10, 11, 13) rem sts for the shoulder. Work the other side the same way, reversing shaping.

Front: With smaller needles and Mercury, CO 30 (30, 34, 34) sts for the front of one leg,. Work in k2, p2 ribbing for ⅝ in / 1.5 cm, beg and ending the first and all odd-numbered rows (RS) with k2. Change to larger needles and striped pattern in St st, increasing 0 (1, 0, 0) sts on the first row = 30 (31, 34, 34) sts.

When piece measures 1½ (2, 2½, 2¾) in / 3.5 (5, 6, 7) cm after the ribbing, shape the crotch: at the right edge, on every other row, inc 1 st 3 times and 2 sts once = 35 (36, 39, 39) sts.

When piece measures 2½ (3¼, 3½, 4) in / 6.5 (8, 9, 10) cm after the ribbing, sl sts to a holder. Work the front of the other leg the same way, reversing the shaping.

Working on all 70 (72, 78, 78) sts, dec at each side as follows: 1 st every 12 rows 5 times (1 st every 14th row 2 times and 1 st every 12th row 3 times; 1 st on the 14th row, and then 1 st every 12th row 5 time; 1 st every 20th row 3 times and then 1 st after 18 rows).

At the same time, when piece measures 7 (7¾, 10½, 12) in / 17.5 (19.5, 26.5, 30.5) cm after the ribbing, work on the first 50 (51, 53, 54) sts and slip the sts at the left to a holder.

When piece measures 9 (9¾, 12½, 14) in / 22.5 (24.4, 31.5, 35.5) cm after the ribbing, shape the neckline: at neck edge, BO 2 sts once, and then, on every other row, BO 2 sts 4 times and 1 st 20 times (2 sts 5 times and 1 st 19 times; 2 sts 6 times and 1 st 18 times; 2 sts 6 times and 1 st 18 times).

When piece measures 10½ (11¾, 13¼, 14¾) in / 26.5 (29.5, 33.5, 37.5) cm after the ribbing, shape the armholes: on every other row at each side, BO 3 sts once, 2 sts 2 times, and 1 st once.

23 - Pink and Gray Socks

SIZES
Newborn (3, 6-9) months

MATERIALS
Yarn: CYCA #1, Phildar Phil Coton 3 (100% Cotton, 132 yd/121 m / 50 g), 1 (1, 1) ball Mercury and 1 (1, 1) ball Dew
Needles: U.S. sizes 1-2 and 2-3 / 2.5 and 3 mm
Notions: Stitch holder

GAUGE
With U.S. size 2-3 / 3 mm needles, 26 sts and 35 rows of stockinette or striped stockinette stitch = 4 x 4 in / 10 x 10 cm. Adjust needle sizes if necessary to obtain gauge.

PATTERN STITCHES
-Ribbing: K2, p2
-Stockinette st: Knit on RS, purl on WS
-Ssk: (Sl 1 knitwise) 2 times and knit tog through back loops

INSTRUCTIONS
With smaller needles and Mercury, CO 34 (42, 50) sts. Work 4 rows of k2, p2 ribbing, beg and ending the first and all odd-numbered rows (RS) with k2. Change to Dew and continue in ribbing.
When piece measures 2½ (3, 3¼) in / 6.5 (7.5, 8.5) cm from the cast-on row, change to larger needles and begin the short-row heel as follows: place the 26 (34, 42) sts at the left side of the knitting on a holder and work only on the rem 8 sts to the right. With Mercury, work short rows, with 1 less st worked toward center (inside of work) on every other row 5 times. Now work 1 more st on every other row 5 times. Repeat the short row sequence with the 8 sts at left side of heel.
Change to Dew and continue, working across all the stitches for the foot. When piece measures 1½ (1¾, 2¼) in / 3.5 (4.5, 5.5) cm after the heel, change to Mercury and shape the toe: K7 (9, 11), ssk, k2tog, k12 (16, 20), ssk, k2tog, and k7 (9, 11). Repeat these decreases every other row as established 5 (7, 9) times. Cut yarn, draw through sts, and fasten securely.

FINISHING
Seam the sole and the leg.

24 - Blue and Gray Socks

SIZES
Newborn (3, 6-9) months

MATERIALS
Yarn: CYCA #1, Phildar Phil Coton 3 (100% Cotton, 132 yd/121 m / 50 g), 1 (1, 1) ball Mercury and 1 (1, 1) ball Sky Blue
Needles: U.S. sizes 1-2 and 2-3 / 2.5 and 3 mm
Notions: Stitch holder

GAUGE
With U.S. size 2-3 / 3 mm needles, 26 sts and 35 rows = 4 x 4 in / 10 x 10 cm. Adjust needle sizes if necessary to obtain gauge.

PATTERN STITCHES
-Ribbing: K2, p2
-Stockinette st: Knit on RS, purl on WS
-Ssk: (Sl 1 knitwise) 2 times and knit tog through back loops

INSTRUCTIONS
With smaller needles and Sky Blue, CO 34 (42, 50) sts. Work in k2, p2 ribbing, beg and ending the first and all odd-numbered rows (RS) with k2.
When piece measures 2½ (3, 3¼) in / 6.5 (7.5, 8.5) cm from cast-on row, change to larger needles and Mercury and begin the short-row heel as follows: place the 26 (34, 42) sts at the left side of the knitting on a holder and work only on the rem 8 sts to the right. With Mercury, work short rows, with 1 less st worked toward center (inside of work) on every other row 5 times. Now work 1 more st on every other row 5 times. Repeat the short row sequence with the 8 sts at left side of heel.
Now work across all the sts for the foot. When piece measures 1½ (1¾, 2¼) in / 3.5 (4.5, 5.5) cm after the heel, shape the toe as follows: K7 (9, 11), ssk, k2tog, k12 (16, 20), ssk, k2tog, and k7 (9, 11). Repeat these decreases every other row as established 5 (7, 9) times. Cut yarn, draw through sts and fasten securely.

FINISHING
Seam the sole and the leg.

25, 26 & 27
Hat, Sweater, and Booties

A very sweet, easy-to-knit outfit in garter stitch, decorated with small mother-of-pearl buttons. Pilou yarn. U.S. sizes 6 and 8 / 4 and 5 mm needles.

25 - *Hat*

SIZES
1 to 3 (6) months

MATERIALS
Yarn: CYCA #2, Phildar Pilou (50% Acrylic, 29% Nylon, 13% Wool, and 8% Elasthan, 66 yd/60 m / 25 g), 1 ball Sky Blue
Needles: U.S. size 8 / 5 mm
Notions: 2 buttons

GAUGE
23 sts and 46 rows = 4 x 4 in / 10 x 10 cm. **Note:** The yarn is very stretchy. The swatch should be made several hours before measuring. Adjust needle size if necessary to obtain gauge.

PATTERN STITCHES
-Garter st: Knit every row

INSTRUCTIONS
CO 86 (96) sts and work in garter st. When piece measures 3½ (4) in / 9 (10) cm, begin decreasing to shape the crown as follows:
Size 1 to 3 months: K6, (k2tog, k7) 8 times, k2tog, k6 = 77 sts.
Size 6 months: (K7, k2tog) 10 times, k6 = 86 sts.
Knit 3 rows, then:
Size 1 to 3 months: K5, (k2tog, k6) 8 times, k2tog, k6 = 68 sts.
Size 6 months: (K6, k2tog) 10 times, k6 = 76 sts.
Knit 3 rows, then:
Size 1 to 3 months: K5, (k2tog, k5) 8 times, k2tog, k5 = 59 sts.
Size 6 months: K6, (k2tog, k5) 10 times = 66 sts.
Knit 3 rows, then:
Size 1 to 3 months: K4, (k2tog, k4) 9 times, k1 = 50 sts.
Size 6 months: K5, (k2tog, k4) 10 times, k1 = 56 sts.
Knit 3 rows, then:
Size 1 to 3 months: K4, (k2tog, k3) 9 times, k1 = 41 sts.
Size 6 months: K4, (k2tog, k3) 10 times, k2 = 46 sts.
Knit 1 row, then:
Size 1 to 3 months: K3, (k2tog, k2) 9 times, k2 = 32 sts.
Size 6 months: K4, (k2tog, k2) 10 times, k2 = 36 sts.
Knit 1 row, then:
Size 1 to 3 months: K3, (k2tog, k1) 9 times, k2 = 23 sts.
Size 6 months: K3, (k2tog, k1) 10 times, k3 = 26 sts.
Knit 1 row, then:
Size 1 to 3 months: K3, (k2tog) 9 times, k2 = 14 sts.
Size 6 months: K2tog across = 13 sts.
Knit 1 row, then:
Size 1 to 3 months: K2tog across = 7 sts.
Size 6 months: K1, then k2tog across = 7 sts.
Knit 1 in / 2.5 cm more, cut yarn and draw through rem sts. Pull firmly and fasten securely.
Seam the hat. Turn the brim up 1¼ in / 3 cm. Sew 2 buttons through both thicknesses at the center front to hold in place.

26 - *Sweater*

SIZES

1 (3, 6) months

MATERIALS

Yarn: CYCA #2, Phildar Pilou (50% Acrylic, 29% Nylon, 13% Wool, and 8% Elasthan, 66 yd/60 m / 25 g), 4 (6, 6) balls Sky Blue

Needles: U.S. size 8 / 5 mm

Notions: 6 buttons; stitch holder

GAUGE

23 sts and 46 rows on larger needles = 4 x 4 in / 10 x 10 cm. **Note:** The yarn is very stretchy. The swatch should be made several hours before measuring. Adjust needle sizes if necessary to obtain gauge.

PATTERN STITCHES

-Garter st: Knit every row

INSTRUCTIONS

The sweater is made in one piece beg at the bottom of the back.

Cast on 50 (55, 60) sts. Work in garter st.

When piece measures 5¼ (6, 6¾) in / 13 (15, 17) cm, CO 24 (32, 37) sts at each side for the sleeves = 98 (119, 134) sts.

When piece measures 8¼ (9½, 10¾) in / 21 (24, 27) cm, BO 10 (13, 16) sts at center front and work each side separately. Continue over the sts of the left side; work 2 rows and then BO 5 sts = 39 (48, 54) sts.

When piece measures 9½ (10¾, 11¾) in / 24 (27, 30) cm, work as follows: k3, yo, k2tog, k3, yo, k2tog, and knit rem sts.

When piece measures 9¾ (11, 12¼) in / 25 (28, 31) cm, CO 5 sts at the right side, then slip the 44 (53, 59) sts to a holder.

CO 13 sts and work in garter st for ⅜ in / 1 cm. Make a one-st buttonhole 3 sts from each side. When piece measures ¾ in / 2 cm, CO 5 sts at the left for the neck. On the next RS row, CO 10 (13, 16) more sts and continue working on all sts = 72 (84, 93) sts.

When sleeve measures 7 (8, 8¾) in / 18 (20, 22) cm, BO the 24 (32, 37) sts at the left = 48 (52, 56) sts for the left front.

When piece measures 15½ (17¾, 20) in / 39 (45, 51) cm, on every other row, 2 sts in from the right edge, decrease 1 stitch on every other row 10 times.

When piece measures 17¼ (19¾, 22) in / 44 (50, 56) cm, bind off the rem 38 (42, 46) sts.

Continue working on the sts on hold, reversing all shaping and omitting the buttonholes and the curve at the bottom.

FINISHING

Sew the side and sleeve seams. Cross the left front over the right. Sew 4 buttons to correspond to the buttonholes. Sew the last 2 buttons as decoration at center front, just below the neck.

Sweater (cont.)

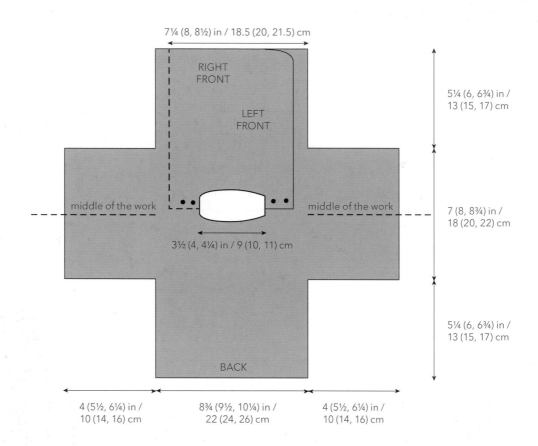

7¼ (8, 8½) in / 18.5 (20, 21.5) cm

RIGHT
FRONT

LEFT
FRONT

middle of the work

middle of the work

3½ (4, 4¼) in / 9 (10, 11) cm

BACK

5¼ (6, 6¾) in /
13 (15, 17) cm

7 (8, 8¾) in /
18 (20, 22) cm

5¼ (6, 6¾) in /
13 (15, 17) cm

4 (5½, 6¼) in /
10 (14, 16) cm

8¾ (9½, 10¼) in /
22 (24, 26) cm

4 (5½, 6¼) in /
10 (14, 16) cm

27 - *Booties*

SIZE

1 to 3 months

MATERIALS

Yarn: CYCA #2, Phildar Pilou (50% Acrylic, 29% Nylon, 13% Wool, and 8% Elasthan, 66 yd/60 m / 25 g), 1 ball Sky Blue

Needles: U.S. size 8 / 5 mm: straight and set of 5 dpn

Notions: 4 buttons

GAUGE

25 sts and 50 rows = 4 x 4 in / 10 x 10 cm. **Note:** The yarn is very stretchy. The swatch should be made several hours before measuring. Adjust needle size if necessary to obtain gauge.

PATTERN STITCHES

-Garter st: Knit every row

INSTRUCTIONS (MAKE 2 ALIKE)

CO 10 sts for the sole. Work in garter st. When piece measures 2¾ in / 7 cm CO 22 sts more at each side for the foot = 54 sts.

Work for ⅝ in / 1.5 cm then cut the yarn. Slip 22 sts to a dpn. Continue working on the 10 center sts, for the top of the foot, and slip the rem 22 sts to another dpn. At the end of each row, knit the last st tog with the first st from the other needle 9 times = 36 sts.

Knit 2 in / 5 cm for the leg and BO.

Seam the back of the bootie and then sew the foot around the sole. Fold the top down toward the outside of the bootie and sew 2 buttons through both thicknesses on the front to hold in place.

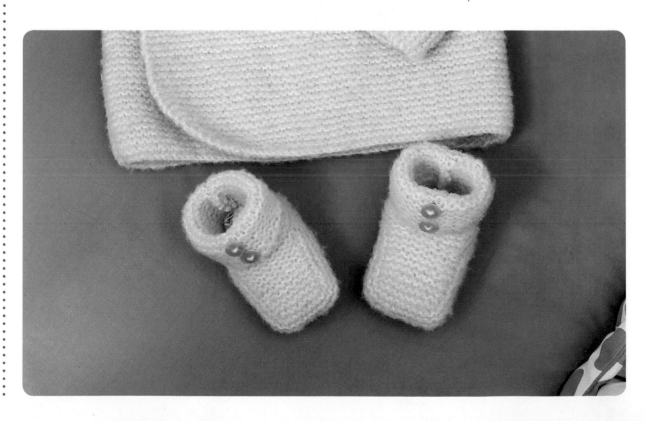

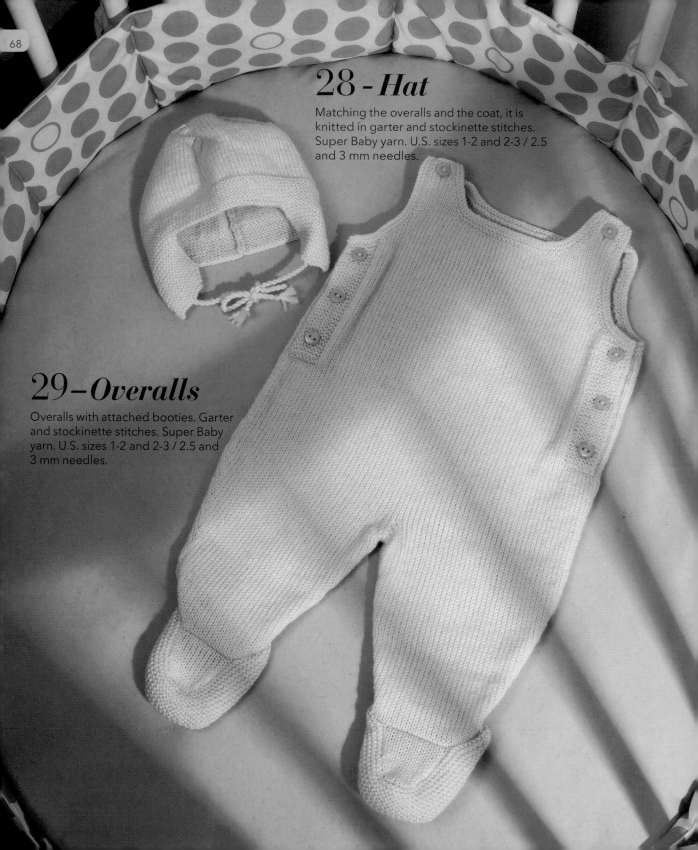

28 - *Hat*

Matching the overalls and the coat, it is knitted in garter and stockinette stitches. Super Baby yarn. U.S. sizes 1-2 and 2-3 / 2.5 and 3 mm needles.

29 – *Overalls*

Overalls with attached booties. Garter and stockinette stitches. Super Baby yarn. U.S. sizes 1-2 and 2-3 / 2.5 and 3 mm needles.

30 - *Coat*

Attractive and warm, it is made with doubled yarn in moss and garter stitch. Super Baby yarn. U.S. size 4 / 3.5 mm needles.

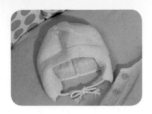

28 - *Hat*

SIZES

1 to 3 (6) months

MATERIALS

Yarn: CYCA #1, Phildar Super Baby (70% Acrylic, 30% Wool, 117 yd/107 m / 25 g), 1 ball Sugared Almond
Needles: U.S. sizes 1-2 and 2-3 / 2.5 and 3 mm; cable needle
Notions: Stitch holder

GAUGE

29 sts and 40 rows on larger needles = 4 x 4 in / 10 x 10 cm in St st. Adjust needle sizes to obtain gauge if necessary.

PATTERN STITCHES

-Garter st: Knit every row
-Stockinette st: Knit on RS, purl on WS
-Dec 3 sts: Work dec on RS. Sl 3 sts to the cable needle and hold behind work; then knit the 1st st on knitting needle tog with the first st on cable needle. Repeat with the 2nd 2 sts and then with the 3rd.

INSTRUCTIONS

With smaller needles, CO 12 sts for one earflap and work in garter st, increasing one st inside each edge stitch on every other row as follows: inc 1 st 4 times, then 1 st once when piece measures 1¾ in / 4 cm. Slip the 22 sts to a holder and make the second earflap the same way. Next, with smaller needles, CO 16 (18) sts for half of the nape of neck, then work the 22 sts of one earflap, CO 30 (34) sts for the front, work the 22 sts of the other earflap, and CO 16 (18) sts for the nape = 106 (114) sts. Work 1 in / 2.5 cm in garter st then change to larger needles and St st. When stockinette measures 2½ (3) in / 6.5 (7.5) cm, begin the bottom as follows: K1 (edge st), (decrease 3 sts, k20 (22) sts) 4 times, k1 (edge st). Work 3 rows without shaping, then: K1, (dec 3 sts, k17 (19) sts) 4 times, k1. Work 3 rows without shaping, then: K1, (dec 3 sts, k14 (16) sts) 4 times, k1. Continue in the same way, working decreases over the previous decreases on every other row until 22 (18) sts rem. K2tog across row. Cut yarn and thread through the rem 11 (9) sts. Draw sts tog and fasten yarn securely. Seam the hat. Make 2 twisted cords. Sew one cord at the bottom of each earflap.

29 - *Overalls*

SIZES

1 (3, 6) months

MATERIALS

Yarn: CYCA #1, Phildar Super Baby (70% Acrylic, 30% Wool, 117 yd/107 m / 25 g), 4 (4, 5) balls Sugared Almond
Needles: U.S. sizes 1-2 and 2-3 / 2.5 and 3 mm
Notions: 8 buttons; stitch holder

GAUGE

29 sts and 40 rows on larger needles = 4 x 4 in / 10 x 10 cm in St st. Adjust needle sizes to obtain gauge if necessary.

PATTERN STITCHES

-Garter st: Knit every row
-Stockinette st: Knit on RS, purl on WS

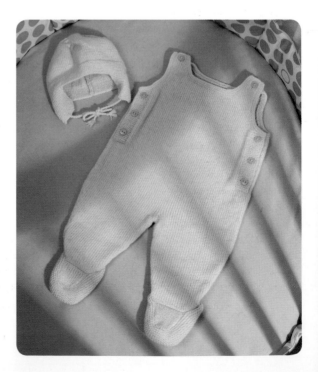

INSTRUCTIONS

The booties are knit separately and then sewn to the bottom of the legs. They may be omitted and a few rows of garter st worked as bottom edges for the legs.

Back: Worked in one piece beg with the bottom of the left leg. Using larger needles, cast on 26 (29, 32) sts. Work in St st, increasing at each side 1 st on every 5th (7th, 8th) row 9 times.

When piece measures 5¼ (6¾, 8) in / 13 (17, 20) cm, slip the 44 (47, 50) sts to a holder.

Work the right leg the same way, then work the sts from the holder = 88 (94, 100) sts.

For the crotch, at each side of the 2 center sts, dec 1 st on every row 3 times, then dec 1 st every other row 2 times = 78 (84, 90) sts.

When piece measures 13 (15, 17) in / 33 (38, 43) cm, begin armhole shaping: at each side on every other row, BO 4 sts once, 3 sts once, 2 sts 2 times, and 1 st 3 times = 50 (56, 62) sts.

When piece measures 15½ (17¾, 20) in 39 (45, 51) cm, BO the 18 (20, 22) center sts and work each side separately. At neck edge, BO 4 sts once, 2 sts once, 1 st 2 times, then 1 st once after 4 rows.

When piece measures 17¾ (20, 22½) in / 45 (51, 57) cm, bind off the 7 (9, 11) sts for the shoulder. Work the other side the same way, reversing shaping.

Front: Work as for the back.

When piece measures 8¾ (10¾, 12¾) in / 22 (27, 32) cm, BO 8 sts at each side for the insets of the button tabs = 62 (68, 74) sts.

When piece measures 13½ (15½, 17¼) in / 34 (39, 44) cm, shape the armholes as follows: at each side, on every other row, BO 2 sts once and 1 st 4 times = 50 (56, 62) sts.

When piece measures 13¾ (16¼, 18½) in / 35 (41, 47) cm, BO the 16 (18, 20) center sts and work each side separately. At neck edge, on every other row, BO 4 sts once, 2 sts once, 1 st 3 times, and after 4 rows, 1 st once.

When piece measures 16½ (19, 21¼) in / 42 (48, 54) cm, make a one-st buttonhole at the center of the shoulder.

When piece measures 17 (19¼, 21¾) in / 43 (49, 55) cm, BO rem 7 (9, 11) sts for the shoulder.

Button tabs: For each of the 2 back tabs, CO 9 sts. Work in garter st for 4¼ in / 11 cm and then bind off. CO 9 sts for each of the 2 front tabs. Work in garter st and make 3 one-st buttonholes at the center: the first when piece measures ⅝ in / 1.5 cm, the others spaced 1¾ in / 4.5 cm apart. When piece measures 4¼ in / 11 cm, at one side, on every other row, BO 4 sts once, 3 sts once, and 2 sts once.

Booties: Made in 2 pieces, the sole with the foot and the top.

For the sole: with smaller needles, CO 14 (16, 18) sts and work in garter st. When piece measures 3 (3¼, 3¾) in / 7.5 (8.5, 9.5) cm, add sts for the foot: at each side CO 30 (33, 36) sts. Continue in garter st on the 74 (82, 90) sts for 1½ in / 3.5 cm and then BO.

For the top of the foot, CO 14 (17, 20) sts and work back and forth in St st until piece measures 1½ (1¾, 1¾) in / 3.5 (4, 4.5) cm. BO 1 st at each side every 4 rows 2 times, then 1 st after 2 rows and 1 st on the next row. BO rem sts.

FINISHING

Place the buttonhole tabs in the insets on fronts. Sew the back tabs at each side of the back at the same height as those of the front.

Armhole Bands (work each side alike): With smaller needles, pick up and knit 50 (53, 57) sts along edge of back armhole. Work 5 rows in garter st and bind off. Repeat on 40 (43, 46) sts of the front armholes.

Neckband: Work as for the armhole bands with 60 (63, 66) sts along back and 58 (61, 64) sts on front.

Sew the side seams. Cross the button tabs of the back under those of the front. Sew the base of tabs down. Sew the leg seams.

Finish the booties by sewing the heel seam. Sew the foot around the sole. Sew the top of the foot to the bootie. Sew the bootie to the bottom of the legs. Sew 3 buttons on each back tab and 1 on each strap.

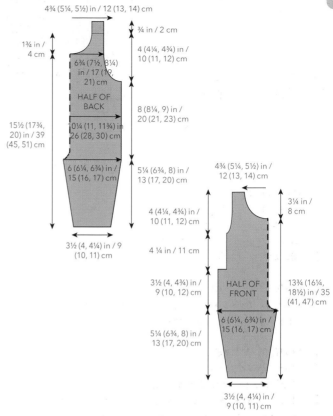

4¾ (5¼, 5½) in / 12 (13, 14) cm

¾ in / 2 cm

1¾ in / 4 cm

4 (4¼, 4¾) in / 10 (11, 12) cm

6¾ (7½, 8¼) in / 17 (19, 21) cm

HALF OF BACK

8 (8¼, 9) in / 20 (21, 23) cm

15½ (17¾, 20) in / 39 (45, 51) cm

10¼ (11, 11¾) in / 26 (28, 30) cm

6 (6¼, 6¾) in / 15 (16, 17) cm

5¼ (6¾, 8) in / 13 (17, 20) cm

3½ (4, 4¼) in / 9 (10, 11) cm

4¾ (5¼, 5½) in / 12 (13, 14) cm

3¼ in / 8 cm

4 (4¼, 4¾) in / 10 (11, 12) cm

4 ¼ in / 11 cm

3½ (4, 4¾) in / 9 (10, 12) cm

HALF OF FRONT

13¾ (16¼, 18½) in / 35 (41, 47) cm

6 (6¼, 6¾) in / 15 (16, 17) cm

5¼ (6¾, 8) in / 13 (17, 20) cm

3½ (4, 4¼) in / 9 (10, 11) cm

30 - *Coat*

SIZES

1 (3, 6) months

MATERIALS

Yarn: CYCA #1, Phildar Super Baby (70% Acrylic, 30% Wool, 117 yd/107 m / 25 g), 6 (8, 8) balls Sugared Almond

Needles: U.S. size 4 / 3.5 mm

Notions: 4 buttons

GAUGE

24 sts and 34 rows in moss st with yarn doubled = 4 x 4 in / 10 x 10 cm. Adjust needle size if necessary to obtain gauge.

PATTERN STITCHES

-Garter st: Knit every row

-Moss st: Row 1: *K1, p1*. Row 2 and all even-numbered rows: Work knit over knit and purl over purl. Row 3: *P1, k1*. Repeat the 4 rows.

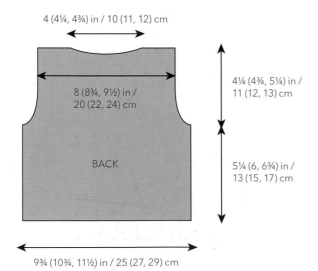

4 (4¼, 4¾) in / 10 (11, 12) cm

8 (8¾, 9½) in / 20 (22, 24) cm

4¼ (4¾, 5¼) in / 11 (12, 13) cm

BACK

5¼ (6, 6¾) in / 13 (15, 17) cm

9¾ (10¾, 11½) in / 25 (27, 29) cm

INSTRUCTIONS

Back: With 2 strands of yarn held together, CO 60 (64, 68) sts. Work in moss st.

When piece measures 5¼ (6, 6¾) in / 13 (15, 17) cm, shape the armholes: at each side on every other row, BO 3 sts once, 2 sts once, and then 1 st once = 48 (52, 56) sts.

When piece measures 9 (10¼, 11¾) in / 23 (26, 30) cm, BO the 12 (14, 16) center sts and work each side separately. Work 2 rows and then BO 6 sts at neck edge.

When piece measures 9½ (10¾, 11¾) in / 24 (27, 30) cm, bind off rem 12 (13, 14) sts for shoulder. Work the other side the same way, reversing shaping.

Right Front: With 2 strands of yarn held together, CO 39 (41, 43) sts. Work in moss st. When piece measures 5¼ (6, 6¾) in / 13 (15, 17) cm, make 2 one-st buttonholes, the first 3 sts from the edge and the 2nd 11 sts from the first. *At the same time*, shape armhole at the left side as for the back = 33 (35, 37) sts. Make a second group of buttonholes 2½ (2¾, 3¼) in / 6 (7, 8) cm from the first. When piece measures 8 (9, 10¼) in / 20 (23, 26) cm, shape neck: at neck edge, on every other row, BO 8 (9, 10) sts once, 4 sts once, 3 sts once, 2 sts 2 times, and 1 st 2 times.

When piece measures 9½ (10¾, 11¾) in / 24 (27, 30) cm, bind off rem 12 (13, 14) sts for shoulder.

Left Front: Work as the right front, reversing all shaping and omitting the buttonholes.

Sleeves: With 2 strands of yarn, CO 32 (34, 36) sts and work for in garter st 1¼ in / 3 cm then continue in moss st, increasing at each side as follows: inc 1 st every 3 rows 10 times (1 st every 4 rows 11 times; 1 st every 4 rows 12 times) = 52 (56, 60) sts.

When piece measures 5¼ (6¾, 7½) in / 13 (17, 19) cm, at each side, on every other row, BO 3 sts once, 2 sts 4 times, and one st once. Bind off rem sts.

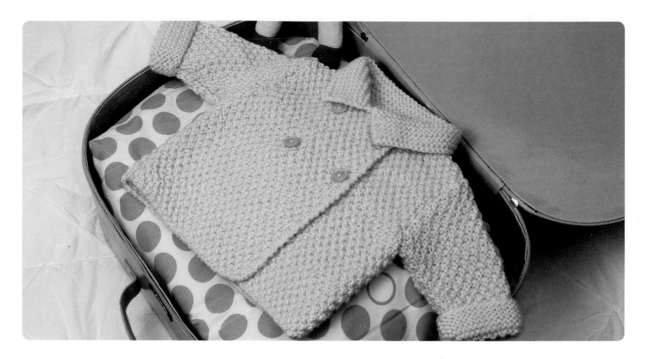

FINISHING

Sew the shoulder seams.

Collar: Cross right front over the left. Place a marker on the neck of each front to indicate the center and then, using 2 strands of yarn, pick up and knit 50 (54, 58) sts around the neck between the markers. Work in garter st for 2 in / 5 cm. BO.

Sew in the sleeves. Sew the sleeve and side seams. Sew on the buttons.

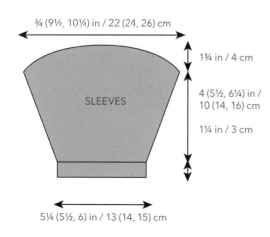

¾ (9½, 10¼) in / 22 (24, 26) cm

1¾ in / 4 cm

SLEEVES

4 (5½, 6¼) in / 10 (14, 16) cm

1¼ in / 3 cm

5¼ (5½, 6) in / 13 (14, 15) cm

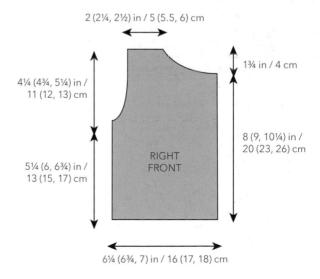

2 (2¼, 2½) in / 5 (5.5, 6) cm

1¾ in / 4 cm

4¼ (4¾, 5¼) in / 11 (12, 13) cm

RIGHT FRONT

8 (9, 10¼) in / 20 (23, 26) cm

5¼ (6, 6¾) in / 13 (15, 17) cm

6¼ (6¾, 7) in / 16 (17, 18) cm

31 & 32 - *Pillows*

Like clouds, very trendy, sweet and decorative;
knit in stockinette st. Pilou yarn. U.S. size 8 / 5 mm
needles.

33 - *Mobile*

Plaything for a baby's crib, made of small clouds in embroidered stockinette st. Pilou yarn. U.S. size 8 / 5 mm needles.

31 - *Blue Pillow*

FINISHED SIZE

Approx. 19¾ x 11 in / 50 x 28 cm

MATERIALS

Yarn: CYCA #2, Phildar Pilou (50% Acrylic, 29% Nylon, 13% Wool, and 8% Elasthan, 66 yd/60 m / 25 g), 4 balls Sky Blue

Needles: U.S. size 8 / 5 mm

Notions: stuffing

GAUGE

25 sts and 39 rows in St st = 4 x 4 in / 10 x 10 cm. **Note:** The yarn is very stretchy. The swatch should be made several hours before measuring. Adjust needle size if necessary to obtain gauge.

PATTERN STITCHES

-Stockinette st: Knit on RS, purl on WS

INSTRUCTIONS

Each side of the pillow is worked following the chart. For example, CO 14 sts. Work in St st, increasing 2 sts at each side of Rows 2 and 3, and 1 st at each side of Rows 4, 5, and 6. The offsets toward the outside correspond to increases, those toward the inside to decreases. Make 1 front and 1 back side. Holding knit (RS) sides together, seam, leaving an opening. Turn piece so the RS is out. Fill with stuffing. Close the opening.

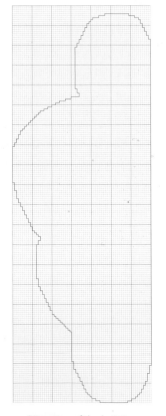 

Direction of the knitting   Direction of the knitting

32 - *Pink Pillow*

FINISHED SIZE
Approx. 13¾ x 7 in / 35 x 18 cm

MATERIALS
Yarn: CYCA #2, Phildar Pilou (50% Acrylic, 29% Nylon, 13% Wool, and 8% Elasthan; 25 g = 66 yd / 60 m), 3 balls Powder
Needles: U.S. size 8 / 5 mm
Notions: stuffing

GAUGE
25 sts and 39 rows in St st = 4 x 4 in / 10 x 10 cm. **Note:** The yarn is very stretchy. The swatch should be made several hours before measuring. Adjust needle size if necessary to obtain gauge.

PATTERN STITCHES
-Stockinette st: Knit on RS, purl on WS

INSTRUCTIONS
Each side of the pillow is worked following the chart. For example, CO 12 sts. Work in St st, increasing 2 sts at each side of Rows 2 and 3, and 1 st at the beginning and 2 sts at the end of Row 4. The offsets toward the outside correspond to increases, those toward the inside to decreases. Make 1 front and 1 back side. Holding knit sides (RS) together, seam, leaving an opening. Turn piece so the RS is out. Fill with stuffing. Close the opening.

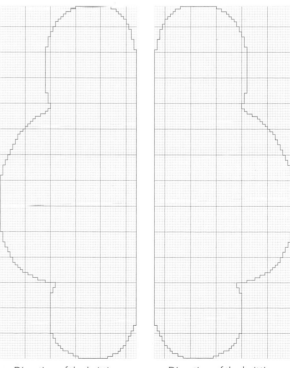

Direction of the knitting   Direction of the knitting

33 - *Mobile*

MATERIALS

Yarn: CYCA #2, Phildar Pilou (50% Acrylic, 29% Nylon, 13% Wool, and 8% Elasthan, 66 yd/60 m / 25 g), 1 ball each of White, Sky Blue, and Powder

Needles: U.S. size 8 / 5 mm

Notions: stuffing; blue and pink embroidery thread; 1 dowel ⅜ in / 1 cm diameter and 15¾ in / 40 cm long, painted white; white satin ribbon 59 in / 150 cm long and ⅜ in / 1 cm wide; glue

GAUGE

25 sts and 39 rows in St st = 4 x 4 in / 10 x 10 cm. **Note:** The yarn is very stretchy. The swatch should be made several hours before measuring. Adjust needle size if necessary to obtain gauge.

PATTERN STITCHES

-Stockinette st: Knit on RS, purl on WS

INSTRUCTIONS

Make 2 small Powder clouds and 2 large Sky Blue clouds, following the charts. Cast on the number of sts corresponding to the first line of the grid. For example, CO 7 sts with Powder for the front side of a small cloud. Work in St st, increasing 1 st at each side of Rows 2, 4, and 6 and 7 sts at each side of Row 10. Offsets toward the outside correspond to increases, those toward the inside to decreases.

For each cloud, make one front side and one back. Holding the knit (RS) sides together, seam, leaving an opening. Turn so that right sides are out. Fill with stuffing and close opening. Embroider the faces (see pictures) with brightly colored embroidery thread.

Make 6 White balls. CO 10 sts. Work in St st, beginning with a purl row on the WS. On Row 2, increase 1 st in each of the 8 center sts = 18 sts. Work 12 rows and, on the next row, k2tog across. Cut yarn and thread through the rem 9 sts. Pull firmly and fasten securely. Fill with stuffing and seam, closing the bottom of 2 balls around the ends of the dowel and completely closing the other 4 balls.

FINISHING

Cut 21¾ in / 55 cm from the ribbon, then 23¾ in / 60 cm to hang the mobile. Thread the 21¾ in / 55 cm length through 1 Sky Blue cloud, 1 ball, one Powder cloud, and 1 ball. Fold the end of the ribbon under the ball and sew in place. Thread 1 ball, 1 Powder cloud, one ball, and one Sky Blue cloud on the 23¾ in / 60 cm length of ribbon. End as for the first length. Fold and sew the free ends of the ribbons around the dowel so that the clouds hang down. Attach the ends of the rem ribbon around the dowel the same way; these ribbons will be used to hang the mobile. Glue the ends of the dowel and slide them into the 2 prepared balls.

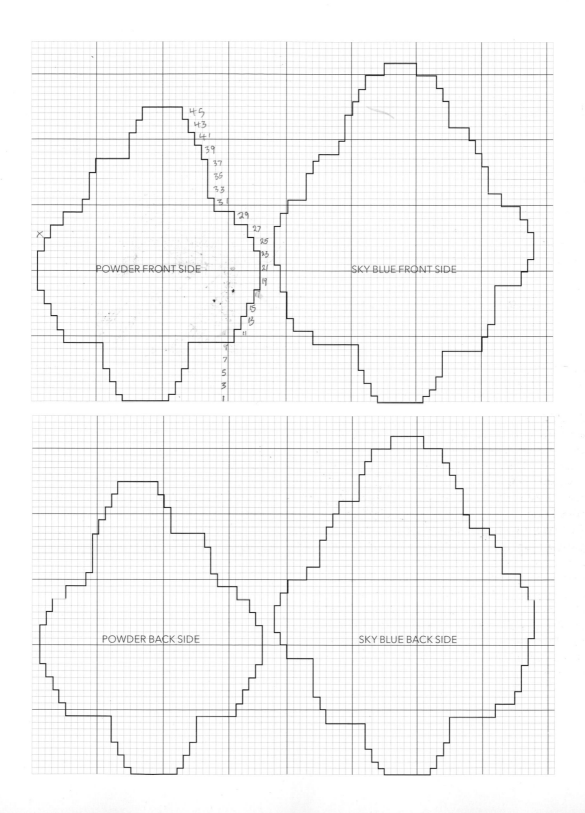

POWDER FRONT SIDE

SKY BLUE FRONT SIDE

POWDER BACK SIDE

SKY BLUE BACK SIDE

Sweet and natural materials; beige, silk, and ecru monochrome.

34 - Angel's Nest

Comfortable and cozy, it is worked in k4, p2 ribbing of stockinette and moss stitches. Closed with big wooden buttons. Rapido yarn. U.S. size 10 and 10½-11 / 6 and 7 mm needles.

35 - *Hat*

Peruvian style, with Fair Isle style design and garter st earflaps, topped with a pompom. Oxygène yarn. U.S. size 2-3 / 3 mm needles.

34 - *Angel's Nest*

SIZE

Newborn to 3 months

MATERIALS

Yarn: CYCA #5, Phildar Rapido (50% Nylon, 25% Wool, and 25% Acrylic, 45 yd/41 m / 50 g), 7 balls Hemp
Needles: U.S. sizes 10 and 10½-11 / 6 and 7 mm
Notions: 3 large buttons and 5 snaps

GAUGE

12 sts and 20 rows in pattern on larger needles = 4 x 4 in / 10 x 10 cm. Adjust needle size if necessary to obtain gauge.

PATTERN STITCHES

-Stockinette st: Knit on RS, purl on WS
-Moss st: Row 1: *K1, p1*. All other rows: knit the purl sts and purl the knit sts
-Ribbing: *4 stockinette sts, 2 moss sts*

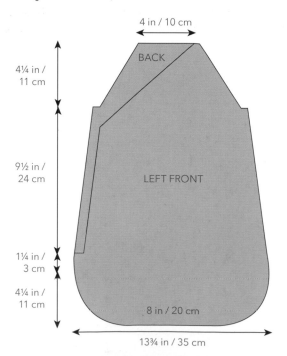

INSTRUCTIONS

Back: Using larger needles, cast on 24 sts. Work in ribbing pattern, beginning with k4. Inc at each side every other row as follows: 3 sts once, 2 sts once, and 1 st 4 times = 42 sts. Continue in pattern as established.
When piece measures 5½ in / 14 cm, decrease 1 st at each side and then 1 st on every 8th row 4 times = 32 sts.
When piece measures 15 in / 38 cm, shape armholes at each side as follows: BO 2 sts once, then after 4 rows, decrease 1 st inside edge st on every other row 7 times.
When piece measures 19¼ in / 49 cm, BO the 14 rem sts for the neck.

Left Front: Begin as for the bottom of the back.
When piece measures 5½ in / 14 cm, work the same decreases on the right side as for the back and, *at the same time*, BO 3 sts at the left edge, then dec 1 st on every 8th row 4 times = 30 sts.
When piece measures 13 in / 33 cm, shape the diagonal at front edge by decreasing 1 st inside edge st on every row 11 times, then, on every other row, dec 1 st 6 times.

When piece measures 15 in / 38 cm, shape the neck, binding off 2 sts at the right side, then after 4 rows, dec 1 st inside edge st on every other row 7 times.

When piece measures 19¼ in / 49 cm, BO rem 3 sts.

Right Front: CO 7 sts. Work the first row of the ribbing pattern as follows: 3 St sts, 2 moss sts, and 2 St sts. Beg with the 5th row, decrease 1 st at the left side every 8th row 5 times. Beg with the 15th row, increase 1 st at the right side every 8th row 2 times = 4 sts.

When piece measures 7½ in / 19 cm, inc 1 st at the right edge on each row 12 times, then inc 1 st on every other row 4 times.

When piece measures 10¼ in / 26 cm, shape the armhole as follows: BO 2 sts at the left side work 4 rows, and then dec 1 st inside edge st on every other row 7 times. *At the same time*, when piece measures 11½ in / 29 cm, decrease 1 st inside edge st at right edge on every other row 7 times.

When piece measures 14¼ in / 36 cm, BO rem 4 sts.

Left Sleeve: CO 20 sts. Work in ribbing pattern, beginning Row 1 with 3 St sts. Inc 1 st at each side every 4th row 5 times = 30 sts.

When piece measures 5½ in / 14 cm, shape the sleeve cap as follows: at

each side, BO 3 sts, then decrease 1 st on every other row 8 times. BO 4 sts at the left side on every other row 2 times. Cut yarn and bring end through rem st.

Right Sleeve: Work as for the left sleeve, reversing all shaping.

FINISHING

Sew the back armholes to sleeve caps then the front armholes. Sew the sleeve seams.

Front Borders: With smaller needles, pick up and knit 47 sts along edge A of the right front. (See right front schematic.) Work 2 rows of k1, p1 ribbing and BO. With smaller needles, pick up and knit 99 sts along the right front neck, back neck, and the diagonal edge of the left front to the split. Work 2 rows of k1, p1 ribbing and bind off. Sew the side seams, sewing the edge st of the ribbing to the 3 bound-off sts of the left front and on the edge st of the left front.

Sew on 3 snaps to close the diagonal, 1 to hold the crossing of the neck in place and the last in the middle of the neck diagonal. Sew the 3 buttons on top of the 3 side snaps.

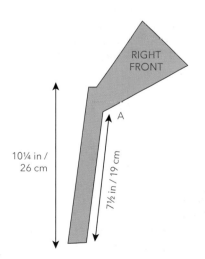

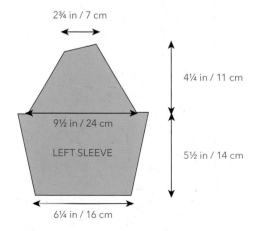

35 - *Hat*

SIZE

1 to 6 months

MATERIALS

Yarn: CYCA #3, Phildar Oxyene (40% Acrylic, 35% Chlorofiber, and 25% Wool, 148 yd/135 m / 50 g), 1 ball each Ecru, Otter, and Reindeer

Needles: U.S. size 2-3 / 3 mm

Notions: Stitch holder

GAUGE

24 sts and 32 rows in St st = 4 x 4 in / 10 x 10 cm. Adjust needle size if necessary to obtain gauge.

PATTERN STITCHES

-Ribbing: K2, p2

-Garter st: Knit every row

-Stockinette st: Knit on RS, purl on WS

-2-color stranded knitting in St st: Follow the chart, being careful to twist the yarns at color changes to avoid making holes

2-color stranded knitting motif

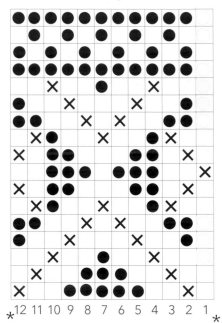

12 11 10 9 8 7 6 5 4 3 2 1

Repeat from * to *

☐ = Ecru

⊡ = Reindeer

⊠ = Otter

INSTRUCTIONS

For one earflap, CO 8 sts using Reindeer. Work in garter st, increasing 1 st at each side every other row 4 times. When piece measures 1¾ in / 4.5 cm, slip the 16 sts to a holder. Make a second earflap the same way.

With Reindeer, CO 12 sts for half of the nape of neck. Work across the sts of one earflap, CO 22 sts for the front, knit across the sts of the 2nd earflap and CO 12 sts for the other half of the nape = 78 sts. Work back and forth in k2, p2 ribbing for ¾ in / 2 cm.

Change to St st, increasing one st at the center of the first row = 79 sts. Beginning with row 3, at the 8th st on the chart, work the 17 rows of the chart. Next, work 3 rows in St st with Reindeer, and then begin crown shaping as follows: K1 (edge st), (k9, k2tog) 7 times, k1 (edge st) = 72 sts rem. Work 3 rows in St st and then decrease as follows: K1, (k8, k2tog) 7 times, k1 = 65 sts. Work 3 rows, then: K1, (k7, k2tog) 7 times, k1 = 58 sts. Continue in the same way, working the decreases over those in the previous rows on every 4th row until 16 sts rem. K2tog across all sts of the next RS row. Cut yarn, leaving a tail of about 6 in / 15 cm, and thread tail through rem 8 sts. Pull firmly and fasten securely. Sew the seam.

Decorate the top with a small Ecru tassel.

36 - Dress

Very graphic, made in stockinette stitch with garter stitch stripes. Cabotine yarn. U.S. sizes 2-3 and 4 / 3 and 3.5 mm needles.

37 - Bag and Booties

The little bag is worked in stockinette stitch and embroidered with twisted cotton. The booties are made in garter stitch with a strap closed by a small wooden button. Lambswool yarn. U.S. sizes 1-2 and 2-3 / 2.5 and 3 mm needles.

38 - Rabbit

Nice and completely round, a big rabbit to cuddle. Made in stockinette stitch. The mouth and eyes are embroidered. Phil Douce and Lambswool yarns. U.S. sizes 2-3 and 8 / 3 and 5 mm needles.

36 - Dress

SIZES

1 (3, 6) months

MATERIALS

Yarn: CYCA #2, Phildar Cabotine (55% Cotton, 45% Acrylic, 136 yd/124 m / 50 g), 3 (4, 4) balls Sand

Needles: U.S. sizes 2-3 and 4 / 3 and 3.5 mm

Notions: 1 button

GAUGE

22 sts and 32 rows in St st on larger needles = 4 x 4 in / 10 x 10 cm. Adjust needle sizes if necessary to obtain gauge.

PATTERN STITCHES

-Garter st: Knit every row

-Stockinette st: Knit on RS, purl on WS

-Pattern sequence: *4 rows garter st, 2 rows St st*

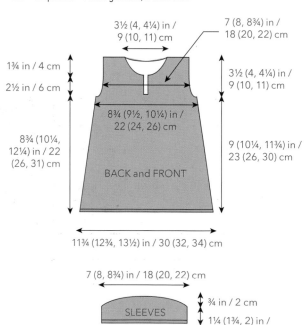

3½ (4, 4¼) in / 9 (10, 11) cm

7 (8, 8¾) in / 18 (20, 22) cm

1¾ in / 4 cm

2½ in / 6 cm

3½ (4, 4¼) in / 9 (10, 11) cm

8¾ (9½, 10¼) in / 22 (24, 26) cm

8¾ (10¼, 12¼) in / 22 (26, 31) cm

9 (10¼, 11¾) in / 23 (26, 30) cm

BACK and FRONT

11¾ (12¾, 13½) in / 30 (32, 34) cm

7 (8, 8¾) in / 18 (20, 22) cm

¾ in / 2 cm

1¼ (1¾, 2) in / 3 (4, 5) cm

SLEEVES

7 (8, 8¾) in / 18 (20, 22) cm

INSTRUCTIONS

Back: With larger needles, CO 68 (72, 76) sts. Work 4 rows garter st, 8 rows St st, 4 rows of garter st, and then continue in St st. *At the same time*, decrease 1 st at each side every 8 (9, 10) rows 9 times = 50 (54, 58) sts.

When piece measures 8¾ (9¾, 11½) in / 22 (25, 29) cm, continue in pattern sequence.

When piece measures 9 (10¼, 11¾) in / 23 (26, 30) cm, beg the armhole shaping. On every other row, at each side, BO 2 sts once and 1 st 2 times = 42 (46, 50) sts.

When piece measures 12¼ (13¾, 15¾) in / 31 (35, 40) cm, BO the 10 (12, 14) center sts and work each side separately. Work 2 rows and BO 5 sts at the neck. When piece measures 12¾ (14¼, 16¼) in / 32 (36, 41) cm, bind off rem 11 (12, 13) sts for shoulder. Work the other side the same way, reversing shaping.

Front: Work as for the back. When piece measures 8¾ (10¼, 12¼) in / 22 (26, 31) cm, bind off the 2 center sts to divide the work into 2 equal parts. Work each side separately.

When piece measures 11 (12¾, 14½) in / 28 (32, 37) cm, at neck edge, BO 3 (4, 5) sts once, 2 sts 2 times, and 1 st 2 times.

When piece measures 12¾ (14¼, 16¼) in / 32 (36, 41) cm, bind off rem 11 (12, 13) sts for shoulder. Work the other side the same way, reversing shaping.

Sleeves: With larger needles, CO 40 (44, 48) sts. Work 4 rows in garter st and then continue in St st. When piece measures 1¼ (1¾, 2) in / 3 (4, 5) cm, on every other row, at each side, BO 1 st 2 times and 2 sts once. Bind off rem sts.

FINISHING

Bands around Neck Placket: With larger needles, pick up and knit 16 sts on the right edge of the front placket. Work 4 rows of St st, and, on the 2nd row, make a 1-st buttonhole 2 sts from the neck edge. BO knitwise on the WS. Repeat for the left edge, omitting the buttonhole. Overlap the bands with right side on top and sew down at base of placket. Seam shoulders.

Neckband: With smaller needles, pick up and knit 60 (64, 68) sts around the neck and tops of placket bands. Work 3 rows in garter st and BO. Sew in the sleeves. Sew the sleeve and side seams. Sew on the button.

37 - Bag and Booties

SIZES

1 (3) months

MATERIALS

Yarn: CYCA #1, Phildar Lambswool (51% Wool, 49% Acrylic, 146 yd/134 m / 50 g), 1 ball Ecru and 1 ball Hemp

Needles: U.S. sizes 1-2 and 2-3 / 2.5 and 3 mm

Notions: 2 buttons

GAUGE

26 sts and 36 rows in St st on larger needles = 4 x 4 in / 10 x 10 cm. Adjust needle sizes if necessary to obtain gauge.

PATTERN STITCHES

-Garter st: Knit every row

Stockinette st: Knit on RS, purl on WS

The designs on the bag are embroidered in chain st.

BAG INSTRUCTIONS

The bag is made in one piece, beginning at the bottom.

With larger needles and Hemp, CO 86 sts. Work in St st until piece measures 6 in / 15 cm. Purl 1 row on the RS. Work 6 rows in St st. Knit 1 row on the WS, then continue in St st. When piece measures 9½ in / 24 cm, BO.

FINISHING

With wrong sides together, fold the bag. Enlarge the design and trace onto tissue paper. Tack onto the knitted piece. Embroider in chain st with Ecru. Carefully remove the tissue paper. Seam the bottom and side of the bag. Fold the top of the bag to the WS on the fold line (see drawing) and fasten the BO row to the lower garter ridge with slip sts. Stitch again on the other garter ridge to make a casing.

With 6 strands of Ecru 39½ in / 100 cm long, make a twisted cord that measures 19¾ in / 50 cm long when folded in half. Thread the cord through the casing, starting at center front, by easing cord between stitches. Knot and trim the ends of the cord.

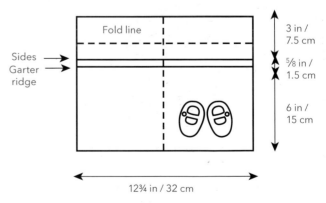

Bag and Booties (cont.)

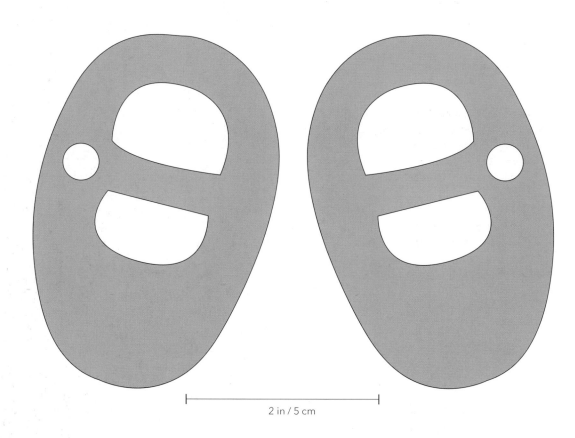

2 in / 5 cm

BOOTIE INSTRUCTIONS

The booties are made in one piece, beginning with the heel of the sole.
With smaller needles and Ecru, CO 12 (14) sts. Work in garter st. When piece
measures 3 (3¼) in / 7.5 (8.5) cm, CO 25 (28) sts at each side for the foot = 62
(70) sts. Knit 6 rows, cut yarn, and then work in garter st on the 8 (10) center sts
for the top of the foot. At the end of each row, k the last st tog with the first st of
those on the sides 14 (15) times. BO the 8 (10) center sts.
Finish each side separately, working over the 13 (15) sts on hold at each side
and casting on 7 (9) sts in the center for the strap. Knit 3 rows on the 20 (24) sts,
making a 1-st buttonhole 2 sts from the edge of one strap. BO.
Make a second bootie, reversing all shaping.

FINISHING

Seam the back and heel of each bootie. Sew on the buttons.

38 - *Rabbit*

DIMENSIONS

About 11¾ in / 30 cm high when it is seated

MATERIALS

Yarn: CYCA #4, Phildar Phil Douce (100% Polyester, 94 yd/86 m / 50 g), 3 balls Ecru and CYCA #1 Phildar Lambswool (51% Wool, 49% Acrylic, 146 yd/134 m / 50 g), 1 ball each Ecru and Hemp
Needles: U.S. sizes 2-3 and 8 / 3 and 5 mm
Notions: Stuffing

GAUGE

15 sts and 27 rows on larger needles with Phil Douce yarn = 4 x 4 in / 10 x 10 cm in St st. Adjust needle sizes if necessary to obtain gauge.

PATTERN STITCHES

-Stockinette st: Knit on RS, purl on WS
-Ssk: (Sl 1 knitwise) 2 times and knit tog through back loops

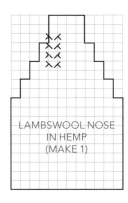

LAMBSWOOL NOSE
IN HEMP
(MAKE 1)

✗ = k2tog

✗ = ssk

Rabbit (cont.)

INSTRUCTIONS

Body: With larger needles and Phil Douce, CO 64 sts and work in St st. When piece measures 7 in / 18 cm, shape the top of the body as follows: K1 (edge st), k6, (k2tog, k13) 3 times, k2tog, k9, k1 (edge st) = 60 sts. Work one row, then continue as follows: K1 (edge st), k6, (k2tog, k12) 3 times, k2tog, k8, k1 (edge st) = 56 sts. Work one row, then on the next row: K1 (edge st), k6, (k2tog, k11) 3 times, k2tog, k7, k1 (edge st) = 52 sts. Decrease the same way on every other row, stacking decreases over those on preceding rows and knitting 1 st less between decreases each time until 28 sts rem. BO.

Bottom of Body: With larger needles and Phil Douce, CO 20 sts. Work in St st for 4¾ in / 12 cm and then BO.

Head: With larger needles and Phil Douce, CO 50 sts. Work in St st. When piece measures 5½ in / 14 cm, shape the crown at the top as follows: K1 (edge st), k2, (k2tog, k10) 3 times, k2tog, k8, k1 (edge st) = 46 sts. Work one row, then continue as follows: K1 (edge st), k2, (k2tog, k9) 3 times, k2tog, k7, k1 (edge st) = 42 sts. Work one row, then: K1 (edge st), k2, (k2tog, k8) 3 times, k2tog, k6, k1 (edge st) = 38 sts. Decrease the same way on every other row, stacking decreases over those on preceding rows and knitting 1 st less between decreases each time until 14 sts rem. BO.

Bottom of the Head: With larger needles and Phil Douce, CO 14 sts. Work in St st for 3¼ in / 8 cm and BO.

Arms (make 4): Use larger needles and work following chart.

Legs (make 4): With larger needles, work according to the chart.

Ears: With larger needles and Phil Douce, make 2 ears following the chart; with smaller needles and Lambswool, make 2 ears following the chart.

Stomach: With smaller needles, work following the chart.

Nose: With smaller needles, work following the chart. The offsets indicate decreases in the center of the work.

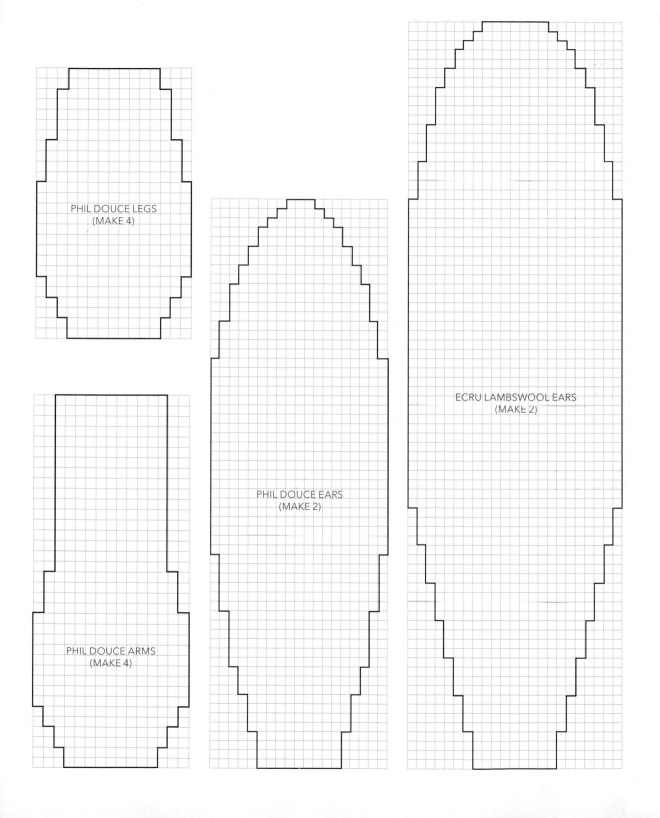

PHIL DOUCE LEGS
(MAKE 4)

PHIL DOUCE ARMS
(MAKE 4)

PHIL DOUCE EARS
(MAKE 2)

ECRU LAMBSWOOL EARS
(MAKE 2)

Rabbit (cont.)

FINISHING

With RS held tog, sew 2 legs, leaving the top open. Turn inside out and stuff. Close the top flat, placing a seam at each side. Repeat with the other leg and the arms.

Close the body into a ball, joining the edge sts and placing the seam at center back. Pin the legs to the front of the body. Sew the body bottom to the body, rounding the angles and including the legs in the seam. Stuff the body.

Close the head into a ball, joining the edge sts. Stuff. Sew the head on its base, rounding the angles. Fasten the head onto the body. Sew the stomach to the body.

Join one ear in Phil Douce and one ear in Lambswool. Sew one ear to each side of the head.

Sew the nose on the front of the head, smaller side down, sliding stuffing in below.

With Hemp, embroider as follows: the eyes and navel in satin st and the mouth in backstitch. Embroider the teeth in satin st with Ecru, outlined with Hemp.

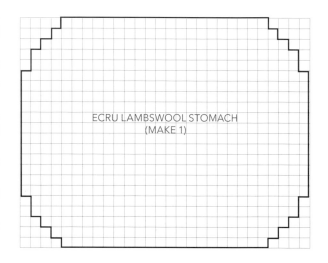

ECRU LAMBSWOOL STOMACH
(MAKE 1)

39 – *Sweater*

Made in stockinette stitch with garter stitch stripes. Closed with big wooden buttons. Iliade yarn. U.S. size 4 / 3.5 mm needles.

39 - *Sweater*

SIZES

3 (6, 12) months

MATERIALS

Yarn: Phildar Iliade (70% Acrylic, 30% Wool, 92 yd/84 m / 50 g), 3 (4, 4) balls Flax

Needles: U.S. size 4 / 3.5 mm

Notions: 3 buttons

GAUGE

19 sts and 40 rows in pattern = 4 x 4 in / 10 x 10 cm. Adjust needle size if necessary to obtain gauge.

PATTERN STITCHES

-Garter stitch: Knit every row

-Stockinette stitch: Knit on RS, purl on WS

-Pattern sequence: *Work 4 rows in garter st, 2 rows in stockinette st*

INSTRUCTIONS

Back: CO 48 (52, 56) sts and work in pattern sequence.

When piece measures 4¼ (5¼, 6) in / 11 (13, 15) cm, CO 14 (17, 20) more sts at each side for the sleeves = 76 (86, 96) sts. Work the 5 sts at each side in garter st for the sleeve edges.

When piece measures 8¼ (9½, 10¾) in / 21 (24, 27) cm, BO the 10 (12, 14) center sts and work each side separately. After 2 rows, bind off 5 sts at neck edge.

When piece measures 8¾ (9¾, 11) in / 22 (25, 28) cm, BO rem 28 (32, 36) sts at the top of the arm and shoulder.

Right Front: CO 24 (26, 28) sts. Work 5 sts in garter st for the front band, 19 (21, 23) sts in pattern sequence.

When piece measures 4¼ (5¼, 6) in / 11 (13, 15) cm, CO 14 (17, 20) sts at the left for the sleeve = 38 (43, 48) sts. Work the 5 sts at the left in garter st for the sleeve edge.

When piece measures 7 (8¼, 9) in / 18 (21, 23) cm, shape neck: on every other row at neck edge, BO 4 (5, 6) sts once, 3 sts once, and 1 st 3 times.

When piece measures 8¾ (9¾, 11) in / 22 (25, 28) cm, bind off rem 28 (32, 36) sts at the top of the arm and shoulder.

Left Front: Work left front as for right front, reversing all shaping.

FINISHING

Sew the seams at the shoulders and top of the arms. Sew the sleeve and side seams.

Neckband: Pick up and knit 52 (56, 60) sts around the neck. Work 3 rows of garter st and BO.

Sew the 3 buttons at the edge of the left front, with the first at the neck and the other 2 spaced 1¾ (1¾, 2) in / 4 (4.5, 5) cm apart. Sew 3 small button loops on right front edge.

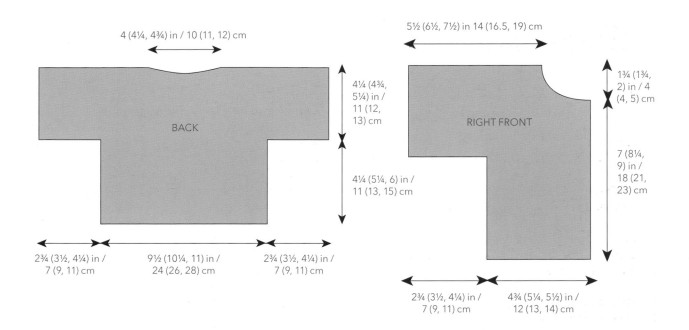

4 (4¼, 4¾) in / 10 (11, 12) cm

BACK

4¼ (4¾, 5¼) in / 11 (12, 13) cm

4¼ (5¼, 6) in / 11 (13, 15) cm

2¾ (3½, 4¼) in / 7 (9, 11) cm

9½ (10¼, 11) in / 24 (26, 28) cm

2¾ (3½, 4¼) in / 7 (9, 11) cm

5½ (6½, 7½) in 14 (16.5, 19) cm

RIGHT FRONT

1¾ (1¾, 2) in / 4 (4, 5) cm

7 (8¼, 9) in / 18 (21, 23) cm

2¾ (3½, 4¼) in / 7 (9, 11) cm

4¾ (5¼, 5½) in / 12 (13, 14) cm

40 & 41 - *Short-sleeved Sailor Top and Socks*

Cute sailor top, short-sleeved version and little matching socks. In stockinette and garter stitches and ribbing. Phil Écolo yarn. U.S. sizes 4 and 6 / 3.5 and 4 mm needles.

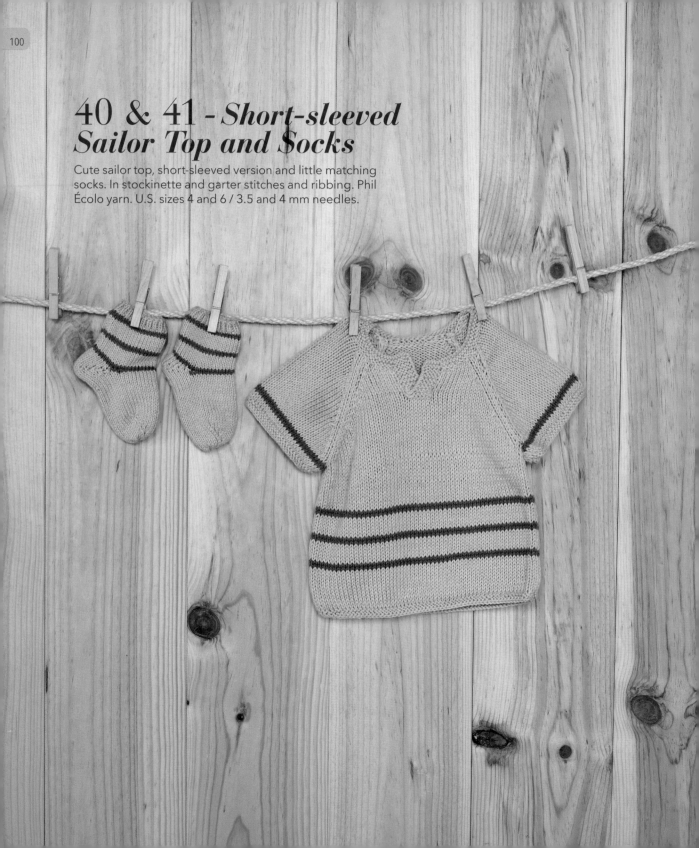

42 & 43 - *Long-sleeved Sailor Top and Socks*

Long-sleeved version and little matching socks. In stockinette and garter stitches, and ribbing. Phil Écolo yarn. U.S. sizes 4 and 6 / 3.5 and 4 mm needles.

40 - *Short-sleeved Sailor Top*

SIZES

6 (12, 18, 24) months

MATERIALS

Yarn: CYCA #3, Phildar Phil Écolo (100% Polyester, 105 yds/96 m / 50 g), 2 (3, 3, 3) balls Sherbet and 1 ball Terracotta; scrap yarn in a contrasting color (used for bands)

Needles: U.S. sizes 4 and 6 / 3.5 and 4 mm; cable needle (for working double decreases)

Notions: Stitch holder

GAUGE

21 sts and 28 rows in St st or striped St st on larger needles = 4 x 4 in / 10 x 10 cm. Adjust needle sizes if necessary to obtain gauge.

PATTERN STITCHES

-Garter st: Knit every row

-Stockinette st: Knit on RS, purl on WS

-Stockinette stripes for the front and back: (2 rows Terracotta, 6 rows Sherbet) 2 times and end with 2 rows Terracotta (18 rows total)

-Single dec 2 sts from the edges as follows: On the right: k2, k2tog; on the left: k to the last 4 sts, ssk, k last 2 sts

-Double dec 2 sts from the edges as follows: On the right: k2, sl 2 sts to cable needle and hold in back, knit the next st from the left needle tog with the first st from cable needle, then knit the next st from the left needle and the last st from the cable needle.

On the left: work to the last 6 sts, sl 2 sts to the cable needle and hold in front, knit the next st from left needle tog with the first st from the cable needle, then knit the next st from the left needle and the last st from the cable needle. Knit the last 2 sts.

INSTRUCTIONS

Back: With smaller needles and Sherbet, CO 56 (60, 64, 68) sts and work in garter st for ⅜ in / 1 cm. With larger needles, continue in St st.

When piece measures 1¼ (1¾, 2¼, 2½) in / 3 (4, 5.5, 6.5) cm after garter st, continue in striped St st pattern. After the 18 rows of the striped pattern, continue with Sherbet.

When piece measures 5½ (6¼, 6¾, 7) in / 14 (16, 17, 18) cm after garter st, shape the raglan: BO 2 sts at each side, then work decreases 2 sts from the edges at each side on every other row as follows:

6 months: (work single dec 3 times, double dec once) 3 times and then work a single dec 5 times at each side.

12 months: (single dec 5 times, double dec once) 2 times and then work a single dec 7 times at each side.

18 months: (single dec 9 times, double dec once) 2 times.

24 months: single dec 10 times, double dec once and single dec 11 times.

When piece measures 10¾ (11¾, 12¾, 13½) in / 27 (30, 32, 34) cm after garter st, loosely BO 12 (14, 16, 18) rem sts.

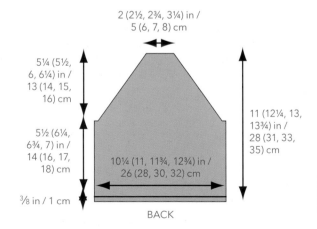

2 (2½, 2¾, 3¼) in / 5 (6, 7, 8) cm

5¼ (5½, 6, 6¼) in / 13 (14, 15, 16) cm

5½ (6¼, 6¾, 7) in / 14 (16, 17, 18) cm

11 (12¼, 13, 13¾) in / 28 (31, 33, 35) cm

10¼ (11, 11¾, 12¾) in / 26 (28, 30, 32) cm

⅜ in / 1 cm

BACK

Front: With smaller needles and Sherbet, CO 56 (60, 64, 68) sts and work in garter st for ³⁄₈ in / 1 cm. With larger needles, continue in St st.

When piece measures 1¼ (1¾, 2¼, 2½) in / 3 (4, 5.5, 6.5) cm after garter st, continue in striped St st pattern. After the 18 rows of the striped pattern, continue with Sherbet.

When piece measures 5½ (6¼, 6¾, 7) in / 14 (16, 17, 18) cm after garter st, shape the raglan: BO 2 sts at each side, then work decreases 2 sts from the edges at each side on every other row as follows:

6 months: (single dec 3 times, double dec once) 3 times and then work a single dec 2 times.

12 months: (single dec 5 times, double dec once) 2 times and then work a single dec 4 times.

18 months: single dec 9 times, double dec once, and single dec 7 times.

24 months: single dec 10 times, double dec once and single dec 8 times.

When piece measures 7½ (8¾, 9½, 10¼) in / 19 (22, 24, 26) cm after garter st, make a neck opening by binding off the 4 center sts and working each

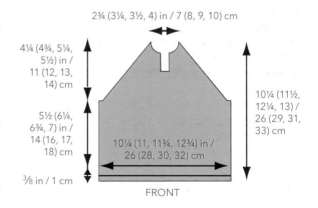

2¾ (3¼, 3½, 4) in / 7 (8, 9, 10) cm

4¼ (4¾, 5¼, 5½) in / 11 (12, 13, 14) cm

5½ (6¼, 6¾, 7) in / 14 (16, 17, 18) cm

³⁄₈ in / 1 cm

10¼ (11, 11¾, 12¾) in / 26 (28, 30, 32) cm

10¼ (11½, 12¼, 13) / 26 (29, 31, 33) cm

FRONT

Short-sleeved Sailor Top (cont.)

side separately.

When piece measures 9 (10¼, 11, 11¾) in / 23 (26, 28, 30) cm after garter st, shape the neck: on every other row at neck edge, BO 2 sts 2 times, 1 st once and 2 sts once (3 sts once, 2 sts once, 1 st once, and 2 sts once; 3 sts 2 times and 2 sts 2 times; 3 sts 2 times and 2 sts 2 times). Work the other side of neck the same way, reversing shaping.

Right Sleeve: With smaller needles and Sherbet, CO 56 (60, 64, 68) sts and work in garter st for ⅜ in / 1 cm. Change to larger needles and continue in St st working 2 rows with Sherbet, 2 rows with Terracotta and finishing with Sherbet.

When piece measures ⅝ in / 1.5 cm after garter st, shape the raglan: BO 2 sts at each side, then work as follows:

6 months: (single dec 3 times, double dec once) 3 times and end with a single dec 2 times.

12 months: (single dec 5 times, double dec once) 2 times and end with a single dec 4 times.

18 months: single dec 9 times, double dec once, and single dec 7 times.

24 months: single dec 10 times, double dec once, and single dec 8 times.

When piece measures 5 (5¼, 5¾, 6¼) in / 12.5 (13.5, 14.5, 15.5) cm after garter st, continue shaping the right side every other row: BO 5 sts once, 4 sts 2 times, and 2 sts once (5 sts 3 times and 2 sts once; 7 sts once, 6 sts once, 5 sts

once, and 2 sts once; 7 sts once, 6 sts 2 times, and 2 sts once).

At the same time, at the left side dec 2 sts from the edge as follows: single dec once and every other row single dec 2 times (single dec once and every other row single dec 2 times; single dec once and every other row single dec once and double dec once; single dec once and, on every other row, single dec 2 times).

Left Sleeve: Make the left sleeve as for right sleeve, reversing all shaping.

Neckband: With smaller needles and Sherbet, CO 70 (76, 82, 86) sts and work in garter st for ⅜ in / 1 cm. Slip the center 60 (66, 72, 76) sts to a holder and work on the 5 edge sts separately, increasing one toward the center = 6 sts.

When piece measures 2 in / 5 cm, knit 1 row on the RS; then, with scrap yarn, work a few rows in St st. Ironing these rows will help in removing them for sewing up.

Continue working on the center sts, ending the same way.

FINISHING

Sew the sleeves to the body along the raglan shaping (with the smallest side at the front). Sew the side and sleeve seams.

With right sides facing, backstitch the neckband in place, putting the 6 end sts on the front opening.

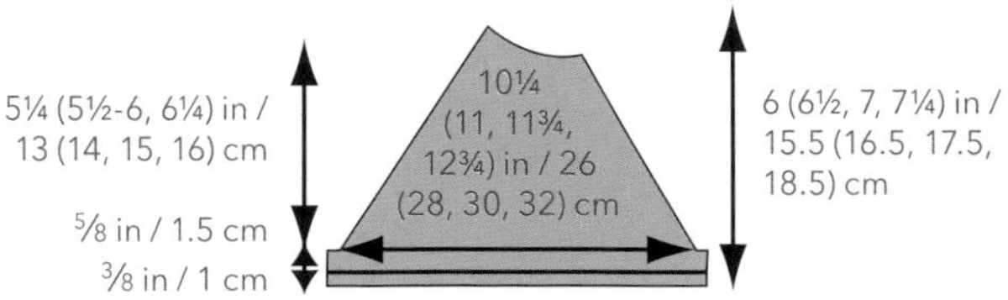

5¼ (5½-6, 6¼) in / 13 (14, 15, 16) cm

10¼ (11, 11¾, 12¾) in / 26 (28, 30, 32) cm

6 (6½, 7, 7¼) in / 15.5 (16.5, 17.5, 18.5) cm

⅝ in / 1.5 cm

⅜ in / 1 cm

RIGHT SLEEVE

41 - *Socks*

SIZES
6 (12, 18) months

MATERIALS
Yarn: CYCA #3, Phildar Phil Ecolo (100% Polyester, 105 yds/96 m / 50 g), 1 (1, 1) ball Sherbet and 1 (1, 1) ball Terracotta
Needles: U.S. sizes 4 and 6 / 3.5 and 4 mm
Notions: Stitch holder

GAUGE
21 sts and 28 rows in St st or striped St st on larger needles = 4 x 4 in / 10 x 10 cm. Adjust needle sizes if necessary to obtain gauge.

PATTERN STITCHES
-Ribbing: K1, p1
-Stockinette st: Knit on RS, purl on WS
-Stockinette stripes: (2 rows Terracotta, 6 rows Sherbet) 2 times and end with 2 rows Terracotta (18 rows total)

INSTRUCTIONS (MAKE 2 ALIKE)
With smaller needles and Sherbet, CO 36 (40, 44) sts and work in k1, p1 ribbing for ⅜ in / 1 cm. Change to larger needles and continue in St st stripes.

After working the 18 rows of stripe pattern, shape the half-heel with short rows as follows: slip the 28 (32, 36) sts at the left to a holder and work with Sherbet on the 8 sts at the right leaving 1 st unworked in the center on every other row 5 times. Then re-work 1 st 5 times every other row and slip the 8 sts to a holder. Repeat with the last 8 sts. Continue working in St st on all sts with Sherbet to form the top of the foot.

When piece measures 1¾ (2, 2¼) in / 4.5 (5, 5.5) cm after the heel, shape the toe as follows: K7 (8, 9), ssk, k2tog, k14 (16, 18), ssk, k2tog, and k7 (8, 9). Repeat the decreases over those of the preceding rows on every other row 4 times. Cut yarn, thread through rem sts, and fasten securely.

FINISHING
Seam the sole and the leg, matching the stripes.

42 - Long-sleeved Sailor Top

SIZES

6 (12, 18, 24) months

MATERIALS

Yarn: CYCA #3, Phildar Phil Écolo (100% Polyester, 105 yd/96 m / 50 g), 3 (4, 4, 4) balls Dolphin and 1 ball Denim; scrap yarn in a contrasting color (used for bands)

Needles: U.S. sizes 4 and 6 / 3.5 and 4 mm; cable needle (for working double decreases)

Notions: Stitch holder

GAUGE

21 sts and 28 rows in St st or striped St st on larger needles = 4 x 4 in / 10 x 10 cm. Adjust needle sizes if necessary to obtain gauge.

PATTERN STITCHES

-Garter st: Knit every row

-Stockinette st: Knit on RS, purl on WS

-Stockinette stripes for the front and back: (2 rows Denim, 4 rows Dolphin) 4 times, and end with 2 rows Denim (26 rows total).

-Stockinette stripes for sleeves: (2 rows Denim, 4 rows Dolphin) 2 times total and end with 2 rows Denim (14 rows total).

-Single decrease 2 sts from the edges as follows: On the right: knit 2, k2tog; on the left: k to the last 4 sts, ssk, k last 2 sts.

-Double dec 2 sts from the edges as follows: On the right: k2, sl 2 sts to the cable needle and hold in back, k tog the next st from the left needle and the first st from the cable needle then the next st from the left needle and the last st from the cable needle.

On the left: work to the last 6 sts, sl 2 sts to the cable needle and hold in front, k tog the next st from the left needle and the first st from the cable needle then the next st from the left needle and the last st from the cable needle. Knit the last 2 sts.

INSTRUCTIONS

Back: With smaller needles and Dolphin, CO 56 (60, 64, 68) sts and work in garter st for ³⁄₈ in / 1 cm. With larger needles, continue in St st.

When piece measures 1¼ (1¾, 2¼, 2½) in / 3 (4, 5.5, 6.5) cm after garter st, work in striped St st. After the 26 rows of the striped pattern, continue with Dolphin.

When piece measures 5½ (6¼, 6¾, 7) in / 14 (16, 17, 18) cm after garter st, shape the raglan: at each side, BO 2 sts and then work decreases 2 sts from the edges every other row as follows:

6 months: (single dec 3 times, double dec once) 3 times and end with with a single dec 5 times.

12 months: (single dec 5 times, double dec once) 2 times and end with with a single dec 7 times

18 months: (single dec 9 times, double dec once) 2 times

24 months: single dec 10 times, double dec once and single dec 11 times.

When piece measures 10¾ (11¾, 12¾, 13½) in / 27 (30, 32, 34) cm after garter st, loosely bind off the 12 (14, 16, 18) rem sts.

Front: With smaller needles and Dolphin, CO 56 (60, 64, 68) sts and work in garter st for ³⁄₈ in / 1 cm. With larger needles, continue in St st.

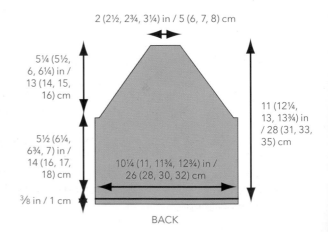

2 (2½, 2¾, 3¼) in / 5 (6, 7, 8) cm

5¼ (5½, 6, 6¼) in / 13 (14, 15, 16) cm

11 (12¼, 13, 13¾) in / 28 (31, 33, 35) cm

5½ (6¼, 6¾, 7) in / 14 (16, 17, 18) cm

10¼ (11, 11¾, 12¾) in / 26 (28, 30, 32) cm

³⁄₈ in / 1 cm

BACK

When piece measures 1¼ (1¾, 2¼, 2½) in / 3 (4, 5.5, 6.5) cm after garter st, continue in striped St st pattern. After the 26 rows of the striped pattern, continue with Dolphin.

When piece measures 5½ (6¼, 6¾, 7) in / 14 (16, 17, 18) cm after garter st, shape the raglan: at each side, BO 2 sts and then work decreases 2 sts from the edges every other row as follows:

6 months: (single dec 3 times, double dec once) 3 times and end with with a single dec 2 times

12 months: (single dec 5 times, double dec once) 2 times and end with with a single dec 4 times

18 months: single dec 9 times, double dec once, and single dec 7 times

24 months: single dec 10 times, double dec once and single dec 8 times.

When piece measures 7½ (8¾, 9½, 10¼) in / 19 (22, 24, 26) cm after garter st, make a neck opening by binding off the 4 center sts and working each side separately.

When piece measures 9 (10¼, 11, 11¾) in / 23 (26, 28, 30) cm after garter st, shape neck: on every other row at neck edge, BO 2 sts 2 times, 1 st once and 2 sts once (3 sts once, 2 sts once, 1 st once, and 2 sts once; 3 sts 2 times and 2 sts 2 times; 3 sts 2 times and 2 sts 2 times). Work the other side of neck the same way, reversing shaping.

Right Sleeve: With smaller needles and Dolphin, CO 38 (40, 42, 44) sts and work in garter st for ⅜ in / 1 cm. Change to larger needles and continue in St st, increasing 1 st at each edge as follows: every 4th row 9 times (every 6th row 2 times then every 4th row 8 times; every 6th row 2 times then every 4th row 9 times; after 6 rows once and then every 4th row 11 times) = 56 (60, 64, 68) sts. *At the same time,* when piece measures ¾ in / 1 cm after

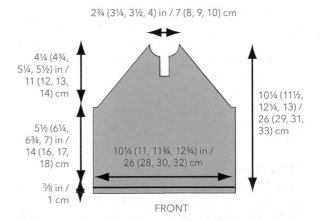

FRONT

Long-sleeved Sailor Top (cont.)

garter st, work in striped St st for 14 rows then continue with Dolphin. When piece measures 5¾ (6¾, 7¼, 7½) in / 14.5 (17, 18.5, 19) cm after garter st, begin the raglan shaping. BO 2 sts at each side and then work decreases 2 sts from the edge stitches every other row as follows:

6 months: (single dec 3 times, double dec once) 3 times and end with with single dec 2 times.

12 months: (single dec 5 times, double dec once) 2 times and end with with single dec 4 times.

18 months: single dec 9 times, double dec once and single dec 7 times.

24 months: single dec 10 times, double dec once and single dec 8 times.

When piece measures 10 (11½, 12½, 13) in / 25.5 (29, 31.5, 33) cm after garter st, continue shaping at the right side on every other row: BO 5 sts once, 4 sts 2 times, and 2 sts once (5 sts 3 times and 2 sts once; 7 sts once, 6 sts once, 5 sts once, and 2 sts once; 7 sts once, 6 sts 2 times, and 2 sts once). *At the same time*, on the left side, dec 2 sts from the edge as follows: single dec once and every other row single dec 2 times (single dec once and every other row single dec 2 times; single dec once and every other row single dec once and double dec once; single dec once and every other row single dec 2 times).

Left Sleeve: Make the left sleeve as for the right sleeve, reversing all shaping.

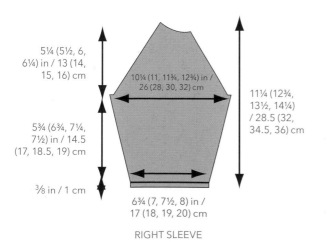

5¼ (5½, 6, 6¼) in / 13 (14, 15, 16) cm

10¼ (11, 11¾, 12¾) in / 26 (28, 30, 32) cm

11¼ (12¾, 13½, 14¼) / 28.5 (32, 34.5, 36) cm

5¾ (6¾, 7¼, 7½) in / 14.5 (17, 18.5, 19) cm

⅜ in / 1 cm

6¾ (7, 7½, 8) in / 17 (18, 19, 20) cm

RIGHT SLEEVE

Neckband: With smaller needles and Dolphin, CO 70 (76, 82, 86) sts and work in garter st for ⅜ in / 1 cm. Slip the center 60 (66, 72, 76) sts to a holder and work on the 5 edge sts separately, increasing one at center front = 6 sts. When piece measures 2 in / 5 cm, knit 1 row on the RS and then, with scrap yarn, work a few rows in St st. Ironing these rows will help in removing them for sewing up.

Continue working on the center sts and end the same way.

FINISHING

Sew the sleeves to the body along the raglan shaping (with the smallest side at the front). Sew the side and sleeve seams.

With right sides facing, backstitch the neckband in place, putting the 6 end sts on the front opening.

43 - *Socks*

SIZES

6 (12, 18) months

MATERIALS

Yarn: CYCA #3, Phildar Phil Écolo (100% Polyester, 105 yd/96 m / 50 g), 1 (1, 1) ball Dolphin and 1 (1, 1) ball Denim
Needles: U.S. sizes 4 and 6 / 3.5 and 4 mm
Notions: Stitch holder

GAUGE

21 sts and 28 rows in St st or striped St st on larger needles = 4 x 4 in / 10 x 10 cm. Adjust needle size if necessary to obtain gauge.

PATTERN STITCHES

-Ribbing: K1, p1
-Stockinette st: Knit on RS, purl on WS
-Stockinette stripes: (2 rows Denim, 4 rows Dolphin) 3 times (18 rows total)

INSTRUCTIONS (MAKE 2 ALIKE)

With smaller needles and Dolphin, CO 36 (40, 44) sts and work in k1, p1 ribbing for ⅜ in / 1 cm. Change to larger needles and continue in St st stripes.

After working the 18 rows of stripes, shape the half-heel as follows: slip the 28 (32, 36) sts at the left to a holder and work with Dolphin on the 8 sts at the right, leaving 1 st unworked in the center on every other row 5 times. Then re-work 1 st 5 times every other row and slip the 8 sts to a holder. Next repeat with the last 8 sts. Continue working St st on all sts with Dolphin to form the top of the foot.

When piece measures 1¾ (2, 2¼) in / 4.5 (5, 5.5) cm after the heel, shape the toe as follows: k7 (8, 9), ssk, k2tog, k14 (16, 18), ssk, k2tog, and k7 (8, 9). Repeat the decreases over those of the preceding rows on every other row 4 times. Cut yarn, thread through the rem sts and fasten securely.

FINISHING

Seam the sole and the leg, matching the stripes.

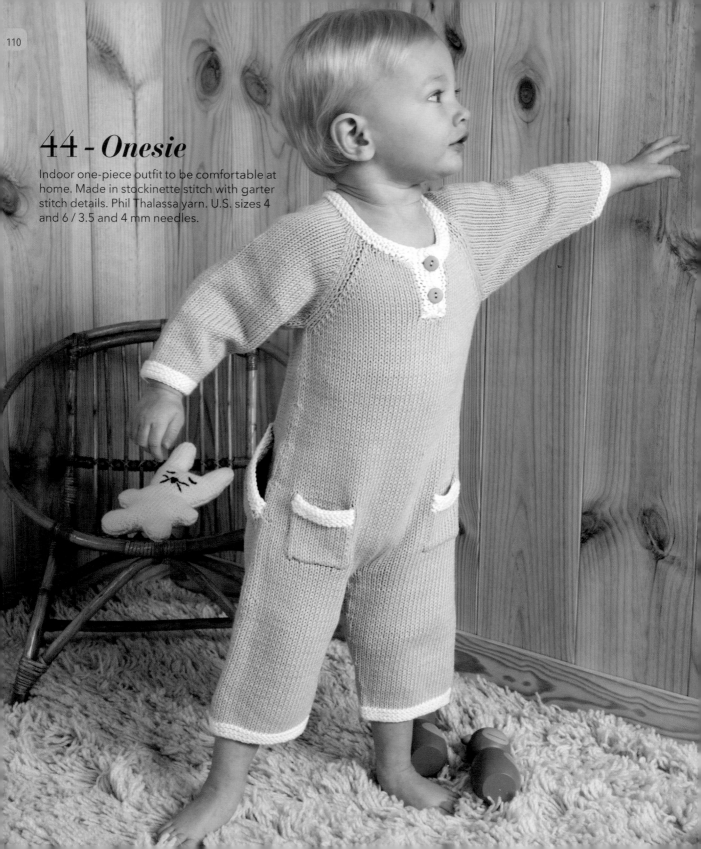

44 - Onesie

Indoor one-piece outfit to be comfortable at home. Made in stockinette stitch with garter stitch details. Phil Thalassa yarn. U.S. sizes 4 and 6 / 3.5 and 4 mm needles.

45
Snuggly Rabbit

Little rabbit to cuddle. Made in reverse
stockinette stitch with garter stitch details.
Phil Thalassa yarn. U.S. size 4 / 3.5 needles.

44 - *Onesie*

SIZES
6 (12, 18) months

MATERIALS
Yarn: CYCA #3, Phildar Phil Thalassa (75% Cotton, 25% Tencel, 88 yd/80 m / 50 g), 4 (5, 6) balls Beige and 1 (1, 1) ball Ecru; scrap yarn
Needles: U.S. sizes 4 and 6 / 3.5 and 4 mm
Notions: 7 buttons; stitch holder

GAUGE
20 sts and 28 rows in St st on larger needles = 4 x 4 in / 10 x 10 cm. Adjust needle sizes if necessary to obtain gauge.

PATTERN STITCHES
-Garter st: Knit every row
-Stockinette st: Knit on RS, purl on WS
-Dec 2 sts from the edges as follows: On the right: k2, k2tog; on the left: k to the last 4 sts, ssk, k last 2 sts

INSTRUCTIONS
Back: Made in 2 parts.
1st part: For a half leg, with larger needles and Ecru, CO 26 (28, 30) sts and work in garter st for ¾ in / 2 cm (6 rows = 3 ridges).
Change to larger needles and Beige and work in St st. Increase at the right side as follows: 1 st every 8 rows 2 times and 1 st every 6 rows 3 times (1 st every 8 rows 5 times, 1 st every 10 rows 5 times) = 31 (33, 35) sts.
When piece measures 5½ (6¾, 8¼) in / 14 (17, 21) cm after garter st, shape the crotch: at right side, BO 1 st once and, 2 rows later, 2 sts once = 28 (30, 32) sts.
When piece measures 6¼ (7¼, 9) in / 15.5 (18.5, 22.5) cm after garter st, sl sts to a holder.
Make the 2nd half-leg, reversing the shaping.
Join the 2 half-legs = 56 (60, 64) sts.
When piece measures 6¼ (7½, 9) in / 16 (19, 23) cm after garter st, shape the curve by binding off at each side as follows: 1 st once, 1 st every 4 rows 5 times, and then every other row 1 st once and 2 sts 2 times.
When piece measures 10¼ (11½, 13) in / 26 (29, 33) cm after garter st, BO the rem 34 (38, 42) sts.
2nd part: For left half of back, with larger needles and Beige, CO 27 (29, 31)

sts and work in St st, decreasing 1 st at the left edge 1 st from the edge stitch as follows: every 10 rows 2 times and every 8 rows 2 times (every 10 rows 4 times, every 12 rows 3 times and after 10 rows once) = 23 (25, 27) sts.
When piece measures 6¼ (7, 8) in / 16 (18, 20) cm from cast-on row, shape the raglan, binding off at the left side 2 sts once (2 sts once, 1 st once) then dec 1 st 2 sts from the edge stitches every other row 16 (17, 19) times.
When piece measures 11 (12¼, 13½) in / 28 (31, 34) cm from cast-on row, BO the 5 (6, 7) rem sts.
Make the right half of back, reversing all shaping.

Front: Begin with a half leg.
With smaller needles and Ecru, CO 26 (28, 30) sts and work in garter st for ¾ in / 2 cm (6 rows = 3 ridges).
Change to larger needles and Beige and work in St st, increasing at the right side as follows: 1 st every 8th row 2 times and 1 st every 6th row 3 times (1 st every 8th row 5 times; 1 st every 10th row 5 times) = 31 (33, 35) sts.
When piece measures 5½ (6¾, 8¼) in / 14 (17, 21) cm after garter st, shape the crotch: at right side, BO 1 st once and, 2 rows later, 2 sts once = 28 (30, 32) sts.
When piece measures 6¼ (7¼, 9) in / 15.5 (18.5, 22.5) cm after garter st, sl the sts to a holder.

1st PART OF THE BACK

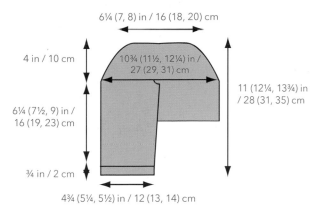

6¼ (7, 8) in / 16 (18, 20) cm

4 in / 10 cm

10¾ (11½, 12¼) in / 27 (29, 31) cm

11 (12¼, 13¾) in / 28 (31, 35) cm

6¼ (7½, 9) in / 16 (19, 23) cm

¾ in / 2 cm

4¾ (5¼, 5½) in / 12 (13, 14) cm

2nd PART OF THE BACK (LEFT HALF-BACK)

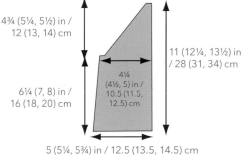

¾ (1, 1¼) in / 2 (2.5, 3) cm

4¾ (5¼, 5½) in / 12 (13, 14) cm

11 (12¼, 13½) in / 28 (31, 34) cm

6¼ (7, 8) in / 16 (18, 20) cm

4¼ (4½, 5) in / 10.5 (11.5, 12.5) cm

5 (5¼, 5¾) in / 12.5 (13.5, 14.5) cm

FRONT

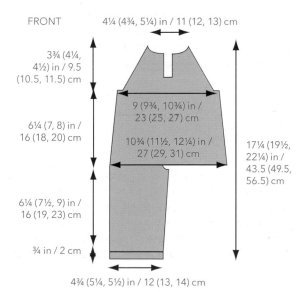

4¼ (4¾, 5¼) in / 11 (12, 13) cm

3¾ (4¼, 4½) in / 9.5 (10.5, 11.5) cm

6¼ (7, 8) in / 16 (18, 20) cm

9 (9¾, 10¾) in / 23 (25, 27) cm

10¾ (11½, 12¼) in / 27 (29, 31) cm

17¼ (19½, 22¼) in / 43.5 (49.5, 56.5) cm

6¼ (7½, 9) in / 16 (19, 23) cm

¾ in / 2 cm

4¾ (5¼, 5½) in / 12 (13, 14) cm

Make the second half leg the same way, reversing all shaping.

Join the 2 half legs — 56 (60, 64) sts and continue in St st.

When piece measures 6¼ (7½, 9) in / 16 (19, 23) cm after garter st, dec 1 st at each side inside edge stitch as follows: every 10th row 2 times and every 8th row 2 times (every 10th row 4 times; every 12th row 3 times and 10 rows later once) = 48 (52, 56) sts.

When piece measures 12¾ (14½, 17) in / 32 (37, 43) cm after garter st, shape raglan: at each side BO 2 sts once (2 sts once; 1 st once) then dec 1 st 2 sts in from edges every other row 12 (13, 15) times. *At the same time*, when piece measures 13 (15½, 18¼) in / 33 (39, 46) cm after garter st, make an opening by binding off the 4 center sts and working each side separately.

When piece measures 15½ (17¾, 20½) in / 39 (45, 52) cm after garter st, shape the neck: at neck edge on every other row, BO 2 sts 4 times (3 sts once and 2 sts 3 times; 3 sts 2 times and 2 sts 2 times). Work opposite side of neck the same way, reversing shaping.

Right Sleeve: With smaller needles and Ecru, CO 30 (32, 34) sts and work in garter st for ¾ in / 2 cm (6 rows = 3 ridges).

Change to larger needles and Beige and continue in St st, increasing 1 st at each side as follows: every 6th row 2 times and every 4th row 6 times (every 6th row 2 times and every 4th row 7 times; every 6th row 3 times and every 4th row 7 times) = 46 (50, 54) sts.

When piece measures 5½ (6¼, 7) in / 14 (16, 18) cm after garter st, shape the raglan: at each side, BO 2 sts once (2 sts once, 1 st once) and then dec 1 st every other row 2 sts from the edges 12 (13, 15) times.

Onesie *(cont.)*

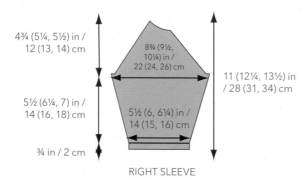

4¾ (5¼, 5½) in /
12 (13, 14) cm

5½ (6¼, 7) in /
14 (16, 18) cm

¾ in / 2 cm

8¾ (9½,
10¼) in /
22 (24, 26) cm

11 (12¼, 13½) in
/ 28 (31, 34) cm

5½ (6, 6¼) in /
14 (15, 16) cm

RIGHT SLEEVE

When piece measures 9¼ (10½, 11¾) in / 23.5 (26.5, 29.5) cm after garter st, continue binding off at the right side on every other row as follows: 3 sts 4 times and 2 sts once (4 sts 2 times, 3 sts 2 times, and 2 sts once; 5 sts once, 4 sts 2 times, 3 sts once, and 2 sts once). *At the same time*, decrease 1 st at the left side and then, on every other row, decrease 1 st 3 times.

Left Sleeve: Make the left sleeve as for right sleeve, reversing all shaping.

Pockets (make 2 alike): With smaller needles and Ecru, CO 14 sts and work in garter st for ¾ in / 2 cm (6 rows = 3 ridges).
Change to larger needles and Beige and continue in St st.
When piece measures 2½ in / 6 cm, loosely bind off all sts.

Button Tabs (make 2 alike): With smaller needles and Ecru, CO 13 sts and work 8 rows of garter st; then, with scrap yarn, work a few rows of St st. Ironing these rows will help in removing them for sewing.

FINISHING

Sew the sleeves to the body along the raglan, with the smaller side to the front. With smaller needles and Ecru, pick up and knit 71 (73, 77) sts around the curve of the back and work in garter st. Make 3 one-st buttonholes on the 3rd row. The first should be 18 sts from the edge and the others spaced 16 (17, 19) sts apart. When piece measures ¾ in / 2 cm, bind off loosely.
Sew the side and sleeve seams.
With smaller needles and Ecru, pick up and knit 42 (46, 50) sts along the left half of back and work in garter st for ¾ in / 2 cm, then loosely BO. Repeat along the right half of back, making 4 one-st buttonholes on the 3rd row. Make the first one 6 sts from the edge at the neck side and space the others 9 (10, 11) sts apart.
With smaller needles and Ecru, pick up and knit 36 sts around the neck and work in garter st, making a one-st buttonhole on the 3rd row 3 sts from the left edge. When piece measures ¾ in / 2 cm, bind off loosely. Repeat on the other side of the neck, omitting the buttonhole.
Sew the button tabs along the front opening.
Sew the pockets 1¼ in / 3 cm above the crotch.
Sew on the buttons.

45 - *Snuggly Rabbit*

MATERIALS

Yarn: CYCA #3, Phildar Phil Thalassa (75% Cotton, 25% Tencel, 88 yd/80 m / 50 g), 1 ball Beige and 1 ball Ecru; a small amount of black cotton embroidery floss

Needles: U.S. size 4 / 3.5 mm

Notions: stuffing; stitch holder

GAUGE

22 sts and 32 rows in St st = 4 x 4 in / 10 x 10 cm. Adjust needle size if necessary to obtain gauge.

PATTERN STITCHES

Knitting:

-Reverse stockinette st: Purl on RS and knit on WS

Embroidery:

-Stem st

-Satin st

RABBIT CHART

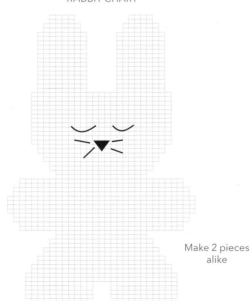

Make 2 pieces alike

= 1 st and 1 row

INSTRUCTIONS (MAKE 2 ALIKE)

Begin with a half leg.

Work following the chart:

With Ecru, CO 5 sts and work in reverse St st, increasing 1 st at each side on every other row 3 times = 11 sts.

On Row 10, slip sts to a holder and make a second half leg.

Join the 2 half legs, casting on 3 sts in the center = 25 sts.

BO 1 st at each side then BO 1 st on every other row 4 times = 15 sts.

On Row 22, shape the arms, casting on 6 sts at each side and then inc 1 st on every other row 2 times = 31 sts.

On Row 30, BO 1 st at each side; then, on every other row, BO 1 st once and 6 sts once = 15 sts.

On Row 36, shape the head: inc 1 st at each side, then, on every other row, inc 1 st 3 times = 23 sts.

Continue working without shaping and, on Row 54, shape the ears, binding off 1 st at each side.

At the same time, BO the 5 center sts and continue each side separately.

On Row 68, BO 1 st at each side, work 2 rows and BO 1 at each side.

On Row 72, BO the 4 remaining sts.

Finish the 2nd ear as for the first, and make the second side as for the first.

Tail: With Beige, CO 2 sts. K4 sts in the 1st st as follows: k1, p1, k1, p1 all in the same st. Drop the 2nd st. Work 7 rows of St st on the 4 sts and then sl 1, k3tog, psso. Cut yarn and thread though the final st, pulling firmly to make a ball.

FINISHING

Sew the seams of the rabbit, leaving an opening so you can stuff it. Stuff and close. Sew the tail in the middle of the back below the arms. Use Black to embroider the eyes in stem st, the nose in satin st, and the whiskers in satin st.

46 & 47
Tunic and Pants

For the stylish, a tunic with coordinating pants.
Made in stockinette and garter stitches. Phil Écolo
yarn. U.S. sizes 4 and 6 / 3.5 and 4 mm needles.

46 - *Tunic*

SIZES
6 (12, 18, 24) months

MATERIALS
Yarn: CYCA #3, Phildar Phil Ecolo (100% Polyester, 105 yd/96 m / 50 g), 4 (4, 5, 6) balls Terracotta; scrap yarn in a contrasting color (used for bands)
Needles: U.S. sizes 4 and 6 / 3.5 and 4 mm
Notions: 2 buttons

GAUGE
21 sts and 28 rows in St st and 21 sts and 33 rows in garter st on larger needles = 4 x 4 in / 10 x 10 cm. Adjust needle sizes if necessary to obtain gauge.

PATTERN STITCHES
-Garter st: Knit every row
-Stockinette st: Knit on RS, purl on WS
-Single dec inside edge sts as follows: On the right: k1, k2tog; on the left: k to the last 3 sts, ssk, k last st

INSTRUCTIONS
Back: With smaller needles, CO 72 (76, 80, 84) sts and work in garter st for ³⁄₈ in / 1 cm. Change to larger needles and continue in St and garter stitches as follows: 3 sts in garter st, 66 (70, 74, 78) sts in St st, and 3 sts in garter st. When piece measures 1¾ in / 4 cm from cast-on row, mark the edge sts and continue in St st for all sts. Dec 1 st at each side inside edge st. Continue decreasing 1 st at each side as follows: every 6th row 7 times and every 4th row 3 times (after 8 rows once and every 6th row 9 times; every 8th row 8 times and every 6th row 2 times; after 10 rows once and on every 8th row 9 times) = 50 (54, 58, 62) sts.
When piece measures 9½ (10¾, 12¾, 13¾) in / 24 (27, 32, 35) cm from cast-on row, work in garter and stockinette as follows: 10 sts in garter st, 30 (34, 38, 42) sts in St st, and 10 sts in garter st.
When piece measures 9¾ (11, 13, 14¼) in / 25 (28, 33, 36) cm from cast-on row, make the sleeves: CO 14 sts at each side (work these sts in garter st) = 78 (82, 86, 90) sts.
When piece measures 12¼ (13½, 15½, 16½) in / 31 (34, 39, 42) cm, continue in garter st for all sts.
When piece measures 14¼ (15¾, 18¼, 19¾) in / 36 (40, 46, 50) cm, shape the neck: BO the 24 (26, 28, 30) center sts and work each side separately.
When piece measures 14½ (16¼, 18½, 20) in / 37 (41, 47, 51) cm, bind off rem 27 (28, 29, 30) sts for the shoulder. Finish the 2nd side of the neck.

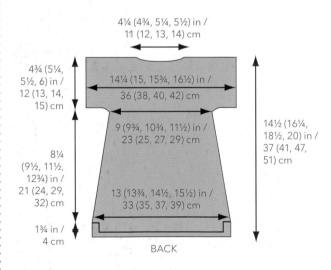

4¼ (4¾, 5¼, 5½) in / 11 (12, 13, 14) cm

4¾ (5¼, 5½, 6) in / 12 (13, 14, 15) cm

14¼ (15, 15¾, 16½) in / 36 (38, 40, 42) cm

9 (9¾, 10¾, 11½) in / 23 (25, 27, 29) cm

14½ (16¼, 18½, 20) in / 37 (41, 47, 51) cm

8¼ (9½, 11½, 12¾) in / 21 (24, 29, 32) cm

13 (13¾, 14½, 15½) in / 33 (35, 37, 39) cm

1¾ in / 4 cm

BACK

Front: Work as for the back to the sleeves = 78 (82, 86, 90) sts.

When piece measures 9¾ (11, 13½, 15) in / 25 (28, 34, 38) cm from cast-on row, make a neck opening by binding off the center 4 sts. Continue working each side separately.

When piece measures 13 (14¼, 16½, 18¼) in / 33 (36, 42, 46) cm from cast-on row, shape the neck: at neck edge, on every other row, BO 3 sts 2 times, 2 sts once and 1 st 2 times (3 sts 2 times, 2 sts once, and 1 st 3 times; 4 sts once, 3 sts once, 2 sts once, and 1 st 3 times; 4 sts once, 3 sts once, 2 sts once, and 1 st 4 times).

When piece measures 14½ (16¼, 18½, 20) in / 37 (41, 47, 51) cm, bind off rem 27 (28, 29, 30) sts for the shoulder. Work the other side of the neck the same way, reversing shaping.

Button Bands: With smaller needles, CO 18 sts. Work in garter st for ⬚ in / 1.5 cm; then, with scrap yarn, knit a few rows of St st. Ironing these rows will help in removing them for sewing.

Make a second band and, on the 5th row make 2 one-st buttonholes. The first should be 4 sts from the edge and the 2nd spaced 6 sts from the first.

Neckband: Using smaller needles, CO 66 (73, 78, 83) sts. Work in garter st for ⅝ in / 1.5 cm; then, with scrap yarn, knit a few rows of St st. Ironing these rows will help in removing them for sewing.

Pockets (make 2 alike): With smaller needles, CO 17 sts. Work in garter st for 2¾ in / 7 cm, then BO loosely.

FINISHING

Sew the shoulder, sleeve, and side seams up to the markers. With right sides facing, backstitch the neckband to the dress, working st by st.

With right sides facing, backstitch the button bands along the front opening and the neckband, working st by st.

Sew the pockets on the front of the dress 1¼ (1¾, 2¾, 3¼) in / 3 (4.5, 7, 8.5) cm from the bottom, spaced 2½ (3¼, 4, 4¾) in / 6 (8, 10, 12) cm apart. Sew on the buttons.

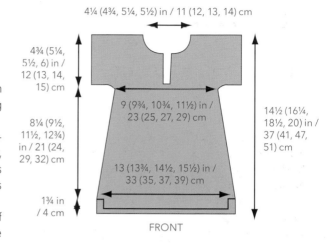

4¼ (4¾, 5¼, 5½) in / 11 (12, 13, 14) cm

4¾ (5¼, 5½, 6) in / 12 (13, 14, 15) cm

8¼ (9½, 11½, 12¾) in / 21 (24, 29, 32) cm

9 (9¾, 10¾, 11½) in / 23 (25, 27, 29) cm

14½ (16¼, 18½, 20) in / 37 (41, 47, 51) cm

13 (13¾, 14½, 15½) in / 33 (35, 37, 39) cm

1¾ in / 4 cm

FRONT

47 - *Pants*

SIZES

6 (12, 18, 24) months

MATERIALS

Yarn: CYCA #3, Phildar Phil Écolo (100% Polyester, 105 yd/96 m / 50 g), 2 (2, 3, 4) balls Sherbet

Needles: U.S. sizes 4 and 6 / 3.5 and 4 mm

Notions: Elastic thread and 2 buttons; stitch holder

GAUGE

21 sts and 28 rows in St st on larger needles = 4 x 4 in / 10 x 10 cm. Adjust needle sizes if necessary to obtain gauge.

PATTERN STITCHES

-Garter st: Knit every row

-Stockinette st: Knit on RS, purl on WS

-Single dec inside edge sts: On the right side: K1, k2tog and on the left: k to the last 3 sts, ssk, k last st

INSTRUCTIONS

Back: Begin with a half leg.

With smaller needles, CO 25 (27, 29, 31) sts and work in garter st for ⅜ in / 1 cm. Change to larger needles and continue in St st and garter st as follows: 22 (24, 26, 28) sts in St st and 3 sts in garter st.

When piece measures 1¾ in / 4 cm from cast-on row, mark the edge st at the left and continue working in St st on all sts.

When piece measures 2½ (3¾, 5¼, 7) in / 6.5 (9.5, 13.5, 17.5) cm from cast-on row, shape the crotch, increasing at the right side on every other row as follows: 1 st once and 2 sts once = 28 (30, 32, 34) sts.

When piece measures 3¼ (4¼, 6, 7½) in / 8 (11, 15, 19) cm, slip sts to a holder. Work the 2nd half leg, reversing all shaping.

Join the 2 half legs = 56 (60, 64, 68) sts.

Dec 1 st at each side, inside edge sts, as follows: after 16 rows once and after 14 rows once (every 16 rows 2 times; after 18 rows once and after 16 rows once; every 18 rows 2 times) = 52 (56, 60, 64) sts.

When piece measures 9¼ (11, 13, 15) in / 23.5 (28, 33, 38) cm from the beg, shape the crotch with short rows. Leave sts unworked at each side every other row as follows: 6 sts 3 times (6 sts 2 times and 7 sts once; 7 sts 3 times; 8 sts 3 times), then work 1 row on all the sts.

With smaller needles, continue in garter st for 1¼ in / 3 cm then BO.

Front: Begin with a half leg.

With smaller needles, CO 25 (27, 29, 31) sts and work in garter st for ⅜ in / 1 cm. Change to larger needles and continue in St. and garter sts as follows: 22 (24, 26, 28) sts in St st and 3 sts in garter st.

When piece measures 1¾ in / 4 cm from cast-on row, mark the edge st at the left and continue working in St st on all sts.

When piece measures 2½ (3¾, 5¼, 7) in / 6.5 (9.5, 13.5, 17.5) cm from cast-on row, shape the crotch, increasing at the right side every other row as follows: 1 st once and 2 sts once = 28 (30, 32, 34) sts.

When piece measures 3¼ (4¼, 6, 7½) in / 8 (11, 15, 19) cm, slip sts to a holder.

Work the 2nd half leg, reversing all shaping.

Join the 2 half legs = 56 (60, 64, 68) sts.

Dec at each side, inside edge sts, as follows: after 16 rows once and after 14 rows once (every 16 rows 2 times; after 18 rows once and after 16 rows once; every 18 rows 2 times) = 52 (56, 60, 64) sts.

When piece measures 9¼ (11, 13, 15) in / 23.5 (28, 33, 38) cm from cast-on row, change to smaller needles and work in garter st for 1¼ in / 3 cm. BO loosely.

FINISHING

Sew the side seams up to the markers. Sew the crotch seams. Weave in several rows of elastic thread around the waist. Sew a button to the bottom of each leg above the 3 sts in garter st.

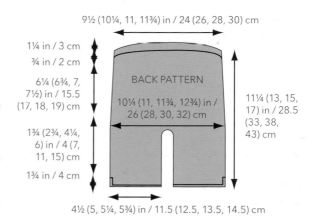

9½ (10¼, 11, 11¾) in / 24 (26, 28, 30) cm

1¼ in / 3 cm
¾ in / 2 cm

6¼ (6¾, 7, 7½) in / 15.5 (17, 18, 19) cm

BACK PATTERN
10¼ (11, 11¾, 12¾) in / 26 (28, 30, 32) cm

11¼ (13, 15, 17) in / 28.5 (33, 38, 43) cm

1¾ (2¾, 4¼, 6) in / 4 (7, 11, 15) cm

1¾ in / 4 cm

4½ (5, 5¼, 5¾) in / 11.5 (12.5, 13.5, 14.5) cm

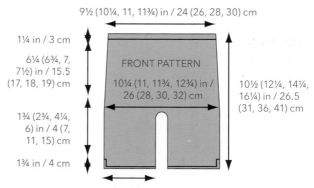

9½ (10¼, 11, 11¾) in / 24 (26, 28, 30) cm

1¼ in / 3 cm

6¼ (6¾, 7, 7½) in / 15.5 (17, 18, 19) cm

FRONT PATTERN
10¼ (11, 11¾, 12¾) in / 26 (28, 30, 32) cm

10½ (12¼, 14¼, 16¼) in / 26.5 (31, 36, 41) cm

1¾ (2¾, 4¼, 6) in / 4 (7, 11, 15) cm

1¾ in / 4 cm

4½ (5, 5¼, 5¾) in / 11.5 (12.5, 13.5, 14.5) cm

48, 49, & 50
Hat, Booties, and Small Bag

Practical: a hat and booties with a little storage bag, a good idea to avoid mislaying them. Made in St st and k2, p2 ribbing. Phil Écolo and Muse yarns. U.S. sizes 2-3, 4, and 6 / 3, 3.5, and 4 mm needles.

48 - *Hat*

SIZES
Newborn (3, 6-9) months

MATERIALS
Yarn: CYCA #2, Phildar Muse (50% Cotton, 28% Linen, 22% Tencel, 121 yd/111 m/ 50 g), 1 ball Nutmeg

Needles: U. S. sizes 4 and 6 / 3.5 and 4 mm

GAUGE
21 sts and 28 rows in St st on larger needles = 4 x 4 in / 10 x 10 cm. Adjust needle sizes if necessary to obtain gauge.

PATTERN STITCHES
-Ribbing: K2, p2
-Stockinette: Knit on RS, purl on WS
-Ssk: (Slip 1 st knitwise) 2 times, knit tog in back loops
-K2tog

INSTRUCTIONS
With smaller needles, CO 78 (82, 86) sts and work in k2, p2 ribbing for 2½ in / 6 cm, beginning and ending the 1st and all odd-numbered rows (RS) with k2. Change to larger needles and continue in St st until piece measures 2¼ (2½, 2¾) in / 5.5 (6, 7) cm after the ribbing. Dec 8 sts distributed as follows: K8 (9, 10), *k2tog, ssk, k15 (16, 17)*; work from * to * 3 times total, and end with k2tog, ssk, k9 = 70 (74, 78) sts.

Continue decreasing on every other row as follows:

K7 (8, 9), *k2tog, ssk, k13 (14, 15)*; work from * to * 3 times total, and end with k2tog, ssk, k8 = 62 (66, 70) sts.

K6 (7, 8), *k2tog, ssk, k11 (12, 13)*; work from * to * 3 times total, and end with k2tog, ssk, k7 = 54 (58, 62) sts.

K5 (6, 7), *k2tog, ssk, k9 (10, 11)*; work from * to * 3 times total, and end with k2tog, ssk, k6 = 46 (50, 54) sts.

K4 (5, 6), *k2tog, ssk, k7 (8, 9)*; work from * to * 3 times total, and end with k2tog, ssk, k5 = 38 (42, 46) sts.

K3 (4, 5), *k2tog ssk, k5 (6, 7)*; work from * to * 3 times total, and end with k2tog, ssk, k4 = 30 (34, 38) sts.

K2 (3, 4), *k2tog, ssk, k3 (4, 5)*; work from * to * 3 times total, and end with k2tog, ssk, k3 = 22 (26, 30) sts.

K2tog across = 11 (13, 15) sts.

K1, then k2tog across = 6 (7, 8) sts.

Work one row; cut yarn, thread end through sts, draw tightly, and fasten securely.

FINISHING
Seam the hat, turning up 1¼ in / 3 cm for the cuff.

49 - *Booties*

SIZE
Newborn to 3 months

MATERIALS
Yarn: CYCA #2, Phildar Muse (50% Cotton, 28% Linen, 22% Tencel, 121 yd/111 m / 50 g), 1 ball Nutmeg
Needles: U. S. size 2-3 / 3 mm
Notions: 2 buttons; stitch holder

PATTERN STITCHES
-Ribbing: K2, p2

INSTRUCTIONS (MAKE 2 ALIKE)
CO 30 sts and work in k2, p2 ribbing, beginning and ending the 1st and all odd-numbered rows (RS of work) with k2.

When piece measures 1½ in / 3.5 cm, mark the selvedge sts to indicate the cuff.

When piece measures 3¼ in / 8.5 cm, slip 10 sts from each side to a holder and work on the 10 center sts for 1¾ in / 4 cm to shape the top of the foot.

Pick up and continue working on the 10 sts at the right; pick up and knit 10 sts on the first side of the bootie, work across the 10 center sts, CO 10 sts on the 2nd side of the bootie and pick up and continue working on the 10 sts at the left = 50 sts.

Work 8 rows of k2, p2 ribbing as follows: 18 sts of ribbing, k4, 6 sts of ribbing, k4, and 18 sts of ribbing.

Leave the 20 sts at each side unworked and knit on the 10 center sts as follows: at the end of every row, k tog the 10th of the center sts and the 1st of the sts on hold. Continue the same way until 6 sts remain at each side and then BO rem sts.

FINISHING
Sew the sole and heel seams.

Strap: CO 6 sts and work in k2, p2 ribbing for 2¼ in / 5.5 cm, beginning and ending the 1st and all odd-numbered rows (RS of work) with p2. BO. Make a 2nd strap. Sew a strap to the top of each bootie and sew a button on the side (see photo, page 122).

50 - *Bag*

ONE SIZE

MATERIALS
Yarn: CYCA #3, Phildar Phil Écolo (100% Polyester, 105 yd/96 m / 50 g), 1 ball Hemp
Needles: U.S. sizes 4 and 6 / 3.5 and 4 mm
Notions: 21¼ in / 54 cm beige cotton ribbon

GAUGE
21 sts and 28 rows in St st = 4 x 4 in / 10 x 10 cm. Adjust needle sizes if necessary to obtain gauge.

PATTERN STITCHES
-Ribbing: K2, p2
-Stockinette st. Knit on RS, purl on WS
-Ssk: (Slip 1 st knitwise) 2 times, knit tog in back loops

INSTRUCTIONS
With smaller needles, CO 46 sts and work back and forth in k2, p2 ribbing for 2 in / 5 cm, beginning and ending the 1st and every odd-numbered row (RS of work) with k2.

Change to larger needles and continue in St st, making a row of eyelets as follows: *k1, ssk, yo*; repeat from * to * and end with k1.

When piece measures 7 in / 18 cm from cast-on row, work in k2, p2 ribbing, beginning and ending the 1st and all odd-numbered rows (RS of work) with k2.

When piece measures 12¾ in / 32 cm, continue in St st.

When piece measures 14¾ in / 45 cm, make another row of eyelets as follows: *k1, ssk, yo*; repeat from * to * and end with k1.

Change to smaller needles and work in k2, p2 ribbing, beginning and ending the 1st and all odd-numbered rows (RS of work) with k2. When piece measures 19¾ in / 50 cm, bind off loosely.

FINISHING
Fold the bag in half and seam the sides. Make a 5-strand twisted cord so that it is 26½ in / 67 cm long when folded in half. Thread the cord through the eyelets.

51 & 52
Peruvian Hat and Booties

Peruvian hat topped with a large pompom and booties with ties. In stockinette st with garter stitch details. Muse and Phil Thalassa yarns. U.S. sizes 2-3 and 4 / 3 and 3.5 mm needles and double pointed needles U.S. size 2-3 / 3 mm.

53 - Onesie

Good-looking one-piece outfit in garter st with small pockets and wooden buttons. Phil Écolo yarn. U.S. size 2-3 / 3 mm needles and U.S. size 1-2 / 2.5 mm crochet hook.

51 - Peruvian Hat

SIZES
Newborn to 3 months (6 to 9 months)

MATERIALS
Yarn: CYCA #2, Phildar Muse (50% Cotton, 28% Linen, 22% Tencel, 121 yd/111 m / 50 g), 1 (2) balls Nutmeg and CYCA #3, Phildar Phil Thalassa (75% Cotton, 25% Tencel; 50 g = 88 yd/80 m) 1 ball Swimming Pool

Needles: U. S. size 4 / 3.5 mm

Notions: Stitch holder

GAUGE
22 sts and 35 rows in St st = 4 x 4 in / 10 x 10 cm. Adjust needle size if necessary to obtain gauge.

PATTERN STITCHES
-Garter stitch: Knit every row

-Stockinette stitch: Knit on RS, purl on WS

-M1 inc: Lift strand between 2 sts and knit into back loop

INSTRUCTIONS
Begin at one ear.

Using Nutmeg, cast on 7 (9) sts. Work in St st, increasing 1 st at each side on every other row 5 times and one st every 4th row 2 times = 21 (23) sts.

When piece measures 2¼ in / 5.5 cm, CO 3 more sts at the left side and *at the same time*, increase at the right side as follows: 1 st once and 1 st every other row 4 times = 29 (31) sts.

When piece measures 3½ in / 9 cm, slip the sts to a holder.

Make a second ear, reversing all shaping.

Continue as follows: K the 29 (31) sts of the 2nd ear, CO 12 (17) sts, work the 29 (31) sts of the first ear = 70 (79) sts. Continue in St st.

When piece measures 3½ (4) in / 9 (10) cm from cast-on row, dec every 4th row as follows:

K2, k2tog, *k5 (6), k2tog*; work from * to * 9 times, ending with k3 = 60 (69) sts.

K2, k2tog, *k4 (5), k2tog*; work from * to * 9 times, ending with k2 = 50 (59) sts.

K1, k2tog, *k3 (4), k2tog*; work from * to * 9 times, ending with k2 = 40 (49) sts.

K1, k2tog, *k2 (3), k2tog*; work from * to * 9 times, ending with k1 = 30 (39) sts.

K2, *k1 (2), k2tog*; work from * to * 9 times ending with k1 = 21 (29) sts.

On the next RS row, k1 then k2tog across = 11 (15) sts.

On the next RS row, k1 then k2tog across = 6 (8) sts.

On the next RS row, cut yarn, thread through sts, pull firmly and fasten securely.

FINISHING
With Nutmeg, pick up and knit 82 (90) sts around the hat and work 4 rows of garter st. BO loosely. Cut 12 lengths of Nutmeg and braid, combining 4 lengths into each strand. The finished braid should be about 5½ in / 13 cm long. Make a second braid and attach braids to the ears. With Swimming Pool, make a pompom about 2 in / 5 cm in diameter and attach it to the top of the hat.

52 - Booties

SIZE
Newborn to 3 months

MATERIALS
Yarn: CYCA #2, Phildar Muse (50% Cotton, 28% Linen, 22% Tencel, 121 yd/111 m / 50 g), 1 ball Nutmeg and CYCA #3, Phildar Phil Thalassa (75% Cotton, 25% Tencel, 88 yd/80 m / 50 g), 1 ball Swimming Pool

Needles: straight and double-pointed U. S. size 2-3 / 3 mm

PATTERN STITCHES
-Garter stitch: Knit every row
-Reverse garter stitch: Purl every row
-Stockinette stitch: Knit on RS, purl on WS
-M1 inc: Lift strand between 2 sts and knit into back loop
-Eyelet row: See details in instructions

INSTRUCTIONS (MAKE 2 ALIKE)
Beginning with the sole, CO 31 sts with Nutmeg and work 2 rows of garter st. Continue as follows:

Row 3: K1, M1, k14, M1, k1, M1, k14, M1, and k1.

Row 4 and all even-numbered rows: Knit all sts.

Row 5: K2, M1, k14, M1, k3, M1, k14, M1, and k2.

Row 7: K3, M1, k14, M1, k5, M1, k14, M1, and k3.

Row 9: K4, M1, k14, M1, k7, M1, k14, M1, and k4.

Row 11: K5, M1, k14, M1, k9, M1, k14, M1, k5 = 51 sts.

Rows 13 and 14: Knit across.

The sole is now finished. Continue in St st for the foot.

When piece measures 1 in / 2.5 cm after the garter st, shape the top of the foot, decreasing on every other row as follows:

K16, (k2tog) 9 times, k17 = 42 sts rem.

K15, (k2tog) 6 times, k15 = 36 sts rem.

K13, (k2tog) 5 times, k13 = 31 sts rem.

K12, k2tog, k3tog, k2tog, k12 = 27 sts rem.

K12, k3tog, k12 = 25 sts rem.

Make an eyelet row as follows: K1 edge st *yo, k2tog*; rep from * to * across row. Purl one row and then shape the cuff as follows: divide work in half, slipping the first 12 sts to a double pointed needle. Work on 13 sts in reverse garter st, purling tog the 2 first sts, then continue working all the sts with heel sides facing and working tog the first st of the first side and the 12th st of the second side = 23 sts. (**Note:** The first row is difficult to work.) Continue in reverse garter st to shape the cuff, working M1, 3 sts from each edge on every other row 4 times = 31 sts.

When garter st measures 1¼ in / 3 cm, bind off loosely.

FINISHING
For each bootie, sew the sole and heel seams. With Swimming Pool, cut 4 strands of yarn to make a twisted cord with a finished length of about 11 in / 28 cm. Thread the cord through the eyelets.

53 - *Onesie*

SIZES

Newborn (3, 6, 9) months

MATERIALS

Yarn: CYCA #3, Phildar Phil Écolo (100% Polyester, 105 yd/96 m / 50 g), 5 (6, 7, 8) balls Hemp and scrap yarn for bands

Needles: U.S. size 2-3 / 3 mm

Crochet hook: U.S. size 1-2 / 2.5 mm

Notions: 11 buttons and 9 snaps; stitch holder

GAUGE

27 sts and 56 rows in garter st = 4 x 4 in / 10 x 10 cm. Adjust needle size if necessary to obtain gauge.

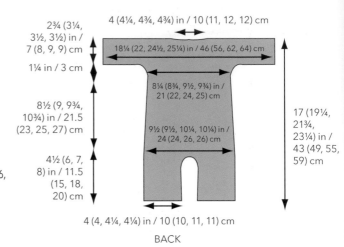

2¾ (3¼, 3½, 3½) in / 7 (8, 9, 9) cm

1¼ in / 3 cm

8½ (9, 9¾, 10¾) in / 21.5 (23, 25, 27) cm

4½ (6, 7, 8) in / 11.5 (15, 18, 20) cm

4 (4¼, 4¾, 4¾) in / 10 (11, 12, 12) cm

18¼ (22, 24½, 25¼) in / 46 (56, 62, 64) cm

8¼ (8¾, 9½, 9¾) in / 21 (22, 24, 25) cm

9½ (9½, 10¼, 10¼) in / 24 (24, 26, 26) cm

17 (19¼, 21¾, 23¼) in / 43 (49, 55, 59) cm

4 (4, 4¼, 4¼) in / 10 (10, 11, 11) cm

BACK

PATTERN STITCHES

Knitting:

-Garter stitch: Knit every row

-Stockinette stitch: Knit on RS, purl on WS

Crochet:

-Slip st (sl st): Insert hook into a st, yarn over and draw it through the loop on the hook

INSTRUCTIONS

Back: Beginning with a half leg, CO 29 (29, 31, 31) sts and work in garter st. When piece measures 3¾ (5¼, 6¼, 7) in / 9.5 (13, 16, 18) cm, shape the crotch: on every other row at the right side, increase 1 st once and 2 sts 2 times = 34 (34, 36, 36) sts.

When piece measures 4½ (6, 7, 8) in / 11.5 (15, 18, 20) cm, slip sts to a holder and make the second half leg, reversing the shaping.

Now work on all 68 (68, 72, 72) leg sts and decrease at each side as follows: 1 st every 20th row 5 times (1 st every 32nd row 3 times; 1 st every 36th row 2 times and 1 st after 34 rows; 1 st after 76 rows) = 58 (62, 66, 70) sts.

When piece measures 13 (15, 17, 18½) in / 33 (38, 43, 47) cm, shape the sleeves: increase 1 st at each side and then, on every other row, inc 1 st 3 times, 2 sts twice, and 3 sts once (22 sts increased). Next, CO 23 (35, 41, 41) sts at each side = 126 (154, 170, 174) sts.

When piece measures 16½ (19, 21¼, 22¾) in / 42 (48, 54, 58) cm, shape the neck, binding off the 10 (12, 14, 14) center sts. Next, work each side separately. Bind off at neck edge, on every other row, 5 sts and then 4 sts.

When piece measures 17 (19¼, 21¾, 23¼) in / 43 (49, 55, 59) cm, bind off rem 49 (62, 69, 71) sts loosely.

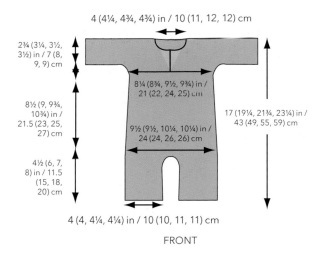

2¾ (3¼, 3½, 3½) in / 7 (8, 9, 9) cm

4 (4¼, 4¾, 4¾) in / 10 (11, 12, 12) cm

8½ (9, 9¾, 10¾) in / 21.5 (23, 25, 27) cm

8¼ (8¾, 9½, 9¾) in / 21 (22, 24, 25) cm

17 (19¼, 21¾, 23¼) in / 43 (49, 55, 59) cm

9½ (9½, 10¼, 10¼) in / 24 (24, 26, 26) cm

4½ (6, 7, 8) in / 11.5 (15, 18, 20) cm

4 (4, 4¼, 4¼) in / 10 (10, 11, 11) cm

FRONT

Front: Beginning with a half leg, CO 29 (29, 31, 31) sts and work in garter st. When piece measures 3¾ (5¼, 6¼, 7) in / 9.5 (13, 16, 18) cm, shape the crotch: on right side, on every other row, increase 1 st once and then 2 sts 2 times = 34 (34, 36, 36) sts.

When piece measures 4½ (6, 7, 8) in / 11.5 (15, 18, 20) cm, slip sts to a holder and make the second half leg, reversing the shaping.

Now work over all 68 (68, 72, 72) leg sts, decreasing 1 st at each side as follows: every 20th row 5 times (every 32nd row 3 times; every 36th row 2 times and after 34 rows once; after 76 rows) = 58 (62, 66, 70) sts.

When piece measures 13 (15, 17, 18½) in / 33 (38, 43, 47) cm, shape the sleeves: increase 1 st at each side and then, on every other row, inc 1 st 3 times, 2 sts twice, and 3 sts once. Next, CO 23 (35, 41, 41) sts at each side = 126 (154, 170, 174) sts.

At the same time, when piece measures 13½ (15¾, 18¼, 19¾) in / 34 (40, 46, 50) cm, divide the work in half and continue on the sts at the right and CO 5 sts at center front (placket). After the sleeve increases, there should be 68 (79, 90, 92) sts.

When piece measures 13¾ (16¼, 18½, 20) in / 35 (41, 47, 51) cm, make a 2-st buttonhole 3 sts from the edge of placket.

When piece measures 15½ (17¾, 20, 21¾) in / 39 (45, 51, 55) cm, make another 2-st buttonhole placed as the first.

When piece measures 15¾ (18¼, 20½, 22) in / 40 (46, 52, 56) cm, shape the neck: at placket edge, BO 9 (7, 11, 11) sts, and then, on every other row, BO 3 sts once, 2 sts 2 times, and 1 st 3 times.

When piece measures 17 (19¼, 21¾, 23¼) in / 43 (49, 55, 59) cm, BO rem 49 (62, 69, 71) sts.

CO 5 sts at center front and, with the sts on hold, work left side as for right side, reversing shaping.

Crotch Bands (make 2 alike): CO 54 (71, 86, 96) sts and work 8 rows of garter st, and then a few rows of St st with scrap yarn. Ironing these rows will help in removing them for sewing.

Pockets: CO 15 sts and work 6 rows of garter st. Continue in St st. When piece measures 2 in / 5 cm, loosely bind off all sts.

CO 20 sts and work 6 rows of garter st. Continue in St st. When piece measures 2 in / 5 cm, loosely bind off all sts.

FINISHING

Sew the seams at the shoulders, sides, and sleeve cuffs. With RS facing, backstitch the bands to the crotch.

Sew the snaps at the crotch and a button over each snap.

Sew 20-st pocket on the right front, ¾ in / 2 cm above the crotch.

Sew the other pocket under the left sleeve (just before the sleeve increases), ⅝ in / 1.5 cm from the edge.

Crochet a row of slip st around the neck. Overlap placket and sew on the buttons.

54 - Hooded Cape

Superb, quick to knit, it is made in moss stitch. Closed with large wooden buttons. Rapido yarn. U.S. sizes 10 and 10½-11 / 6 and 7 mm needles.

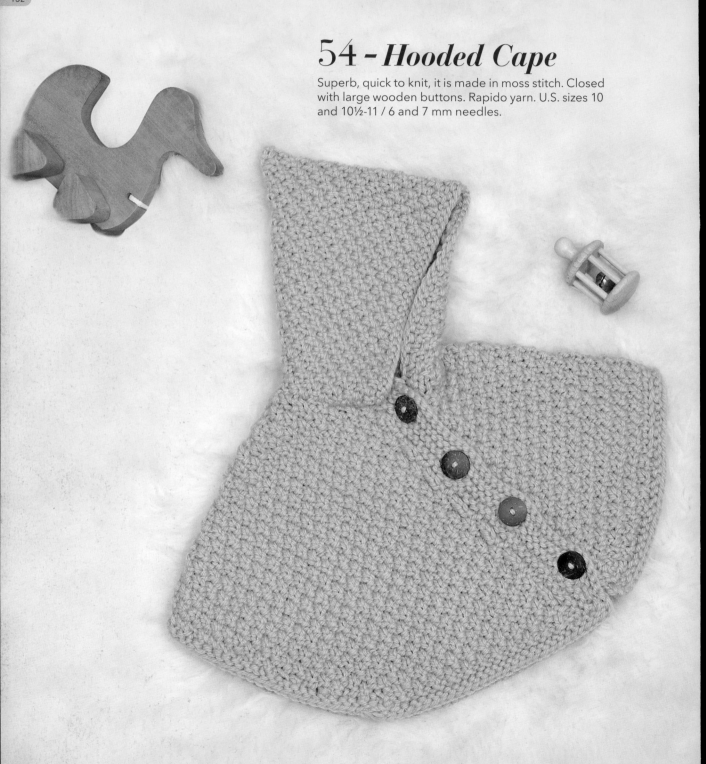

54 - Hooded Cape

SIZES

3 (6, 12) months

MATERIALS

Yarn: CYCA #5, Phildar Rapido (50% Nylon, 25% Wool, and 25% Acrylic, 45 yd/41 m / 50 g), 7 (7, 8) balls Hemp
Needles: U.S. sizes 10 and 10½-11 / 6 and 7 mm
Notions: 4 buttons

GAUGE

13 sts and 20 rows in moss st on larger needles = 4 x 4 in / 10 x 10 cm. Adjust needle sizes if necessary to obtain gauge.

PATTERN STITCHES

-Garter st: Knit every row
-Moss st: Row 1: *K1, p1*. Row 2 and all even-numbered rows: Work the sts as they present themselves. Row 3: *P1, k1*. Repeat the 4 rows for the pattern.

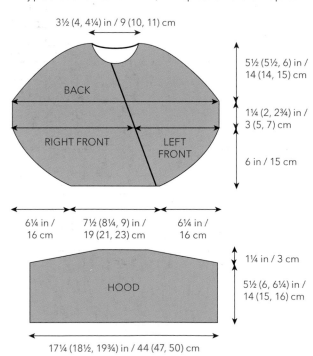

INSTRUCTIONS

Back: With larger needles, CO 25 (28, 31) sts. Work in moss st, following the chart. Each square corresponds to 1 st and 1 row. The offsets toward the outside represent increases and those toward the inside represent decreases.

Right Front: With larger needles, CO 23 (25, 28) sts. Work in moss st, following the chart.

Left Front: With larger needles, CO 2 (3, 3) sts. Work in moss st, following the chart.

Hood: With smaller needles, CO 58 (62, 66) sts. Work 2 rows in garter st then continue in moss st. When piece measures 5½ (6, 6¼) in / 14 (15, 16) cm, BO 8 sts at each side on every other row 3 times. Bind off rem sts.

FINISHING

Button Bands: With smaller needles, pick up and knit 38 (42, 45) sts along edge of left front. Work 6 rows in garter st and BO. Work right front band the same way, but make 4 one-st buttonholes on the 2nd row. The first should be 5 sts from the bottom and the others spaced 9 (10, 11) sts apart.
Sew the tops of the shoulders.

Bottom Edge: With smaller needles, pick up and knit 140 (146, 152) sts around the bottom of the cape and edges of front bands. Work 3 rows in garter st and BO. Fold the hood in half to close the back and sew it at the neck. Sew on the buttons.

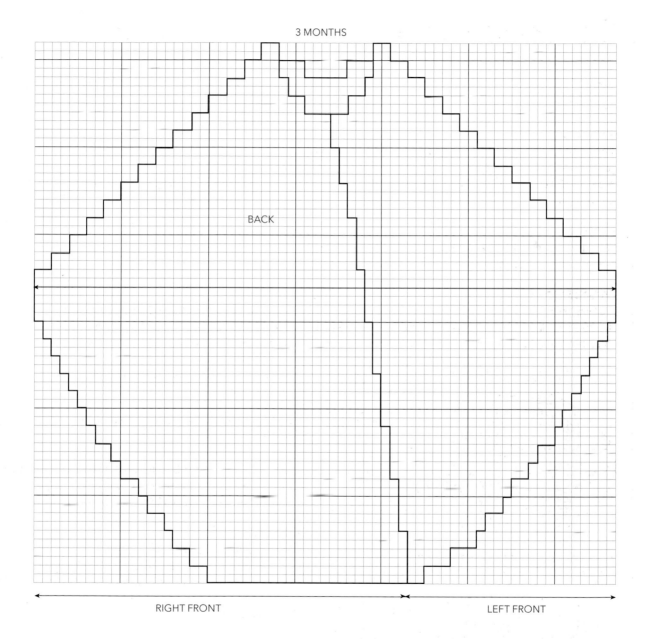

3 MONTHS

BACK

RIGHT FRONT

LEFT FRONT

Hooded Cape (cont.)

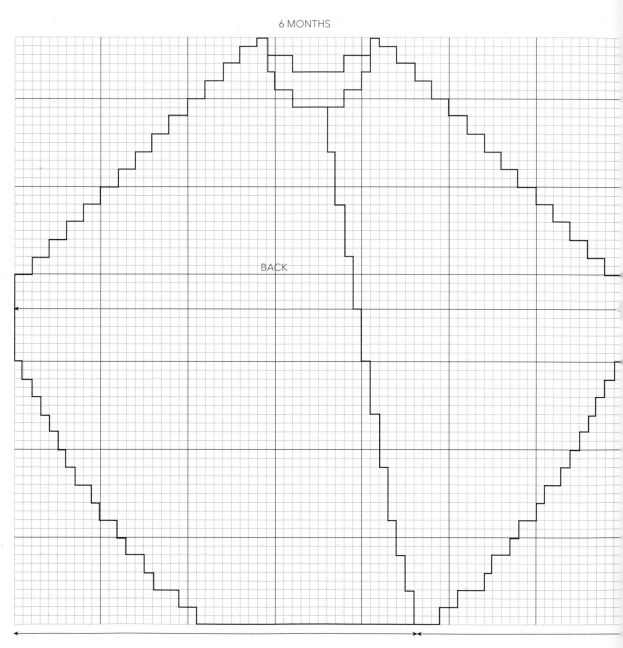

6 MONTHS

BACK

RIGHT FRONT

LEFT FRONT

12 MONTHS

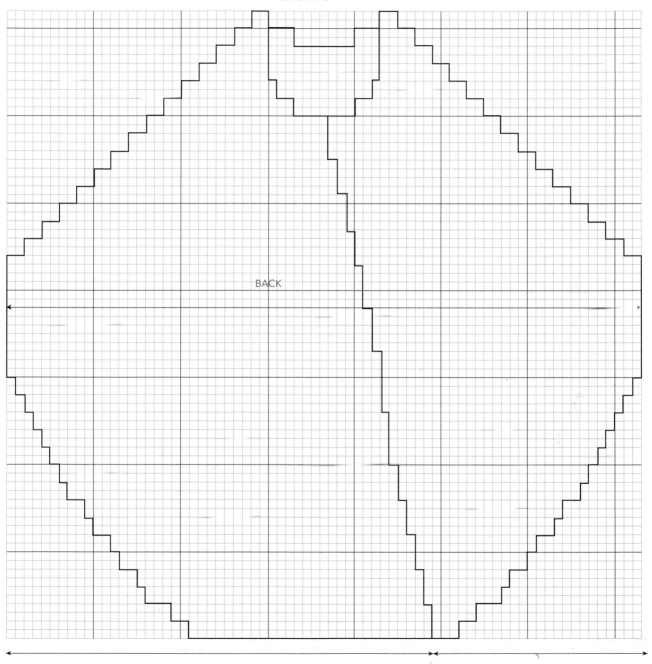

BACK

RIGHT FRONT

LEFT FRONT

*Plum, gray and Liberty;
modern and fanciful.*

55 – Hat

With cables, k2, p2 ribbing, and garter stitch. Partner 6 yarn. U.S. sizes 7 and 8 / 4.5 and 5 mm. Cable needle.

57 - Boots

With cables, k2, p2 ribbing, and garter stitch. Partner 6 yarn. U.S. sizes 7 and 8 / 4.5 and 5 mm. Cable needle.

56 - Coat

Knit in stockinette stitch with reverse stockinette stitch stripes for the sleeves. Partner 6 yarn. U.S. sizes 7 and 8 / 4.5 and 5 mm.

55 - Hat

SIZES

1 to 3 months (3 to 6 months)

MATERIALS

Yarn: CYCA #5, Phildar Partner 6 (50% Nylon, 25% Wool, and 25% Acrylic, 71 yd/65 m / 50 g), 1 ball Slate
Needles: U.S. sizes 7 and 8 / 4.5 and 5 mm; cable needle

GAUGE

With larger needles, 16 sts and 24 rows in St st = 4 x 4 in / 10 x 10 cm. Adjust needle sizes if necessary to obtain gauge.

PATTERN STITCHES

-Stockinette stitch: Knit on RS, purl on WS
-Cables: Row 1: *P2, k4*. Row 2 and all even-numbered rows: Work the sts as they present themselves. Row 3: P2, sl 2 sts to the cable needle and hold in front of work, k2, then k the 2 sts from the cable needle. Row 5: Work as for Row 1. Repeat the 6 rows for the pattern.

INSTRUCTIONS

With smaller needles, CO 62 (66) sts and work back and forth in k2, p2 ribbing for ¾ in / 2 cm. Change to larger needles and continue in cable pattern, increasing 0 (2) sts on Row 1 = 62 (68) sts.

When piece measures 5¼ (6) in / 13 (15) cm, work 5 rows of St st on all the sts and, on the first row, p2tog before and after the cable sts = 51 (56) sts. Change to smaller needles and work 4 rows of k2, p2 ribbing, decreasing 1 (2) sts on Row 1. BO.

Close the top of the hat. Thread a doubled strand of yarn through Row 1 of the stockinette sts. Pull tog as firmly as possible and fasten securely.

CABLES

```
6 | I I I I - -   *
      I I I I - - 5
4 | I I I I - -
      I I I I - - 3
2 | I I I I - -
      I I I I - - 1
  * 6 5 4 3 2 1 *
```

Repeat from * to *

☐ = Knit on RS, purl on WS

⊟ = Purl on RS, knit on WS

✕ = Sl 2 sts to the cable needle and hold in front of work, k2, and then k the 2 sts from the cable needle.

56 - Coat

SIZES

1 (3, 6) months

MATERIALS

Yarn: CYCA #5, Phildar Partner 6 (50% Nylon, 25% Wool, and 25% Acrylic, 71 yd/65 m / 50 g), 5 (6, 7) balls Slate
Needles: U.S. sizes 7 and 8 / 4.5 and 5 mm
Notions: 4 buttons; stitch holder

GAUGE

16 sts and 24 rows in St st on larger needles = 4 x 4 in / 10 x 10 cm. Adjust needle sizes if necessary to obtain gauge.

PATTERN STITCHES

-Ribbing: *K2, p2*
-Stockinette stitch: Knit on RS, purl on WS

INSTRUCTIONS

Back: With smaller needles, CO 46 (50, 54) sts and work in k2, p2 ribbing for ¾ in / 2 cm. Change to larger needles and purl 1 row on the RS, knit 1 row on the WS. Continue in St st, decreasing 1 st at each side inside edge st on Row 20 (26, 34) and then every 12th row 2 times = 40 (44, 48) sts.

When piece measures 8¾ (9¾, 11½) in / 22 (25, 29) cm, shape the armholes, binding off at each side on every other row as follows: 2 sts once and 1 st 2 times = 32 (36, 40) sts.

When piece measures 13½ (15, 17) in / 34 (38, 43) cm, bind off the 16 (18, 20) center sts and finish each side separately. BO for the shoulder on every other row as follows: 4 sts twice (5 sts once and 4 sts once; 5 sts 2 times).

Left Front: With smaller needles, CO 31 (34, 37) sts and work in k2, p2 ribbing for ¾ in / 2 cm. Change to larger needles and continue as for the back (decreases at the right side) = 28 (31, 34) sts before the armhole.

When piece measures 4 (4¾, 6) in / 10 (12, 15) cm, work the pocket band with 4 rows of garter st over 10 (12, 14) sts, placed 14 (15, 16) sts from the left edge (at center front), and keep the other sts in St st. BO the pocket band and slip rem sts to a holder.

Pocket Lining: With larger needles, CO 12 (14, 16) sts. Work in St st for 2½ in / 6 cm, binding off 1 st at each side on the last row. Continue the front, replacing the bound-off sts with those of the pocket lining.

When piece measures 8¾ (9¾, 11½) in / 22 (25, 29) cm, shape armhole at side as for the back = 24 (27, 30) sts.

When piece measures 12¾ (14¼, 16¼) in / 32 (36, 41) cm, BO for the neck at the left side on every other row: 10 (12, 14) sts, 3 sts, 2 sts, and 1 st.

When piece measures 13½ (15, 17) in / 34 (38, 43) cm, BO the shoulder sts in 2 steps as for the back.

Right Front: Work as for left front, reversing all shaping and making a set of 2 buttonholes when piece measures 10¼ (11½, 13½) in / 26 (29, 34) cm and another set when piece measures 12¼ (13¾, 15¾) in / 31 (35, 40) cm. Make the buttonholes as follows: k2, k2tog, yo, k6 (7, 8), k2tog, yo, then knit across row.

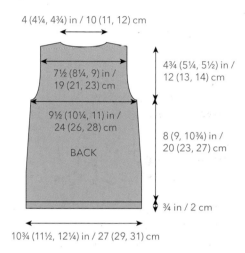

4 (4¼, 4¾) in / 10 (11, 12) cm

4¾ (5¼, 5½) in / 12 (13, 14) cm

7½ (8¼, 9) in / 19 (21, 23) cm

9½ (10¼, 11) in / 24 (26, 28) cm

BACK

8 (9, 10¾) in / 20 (23, 27) cm

¾ in / 2 cm

10¾ (11½, 12¼) in / 27 (29, 31) cm

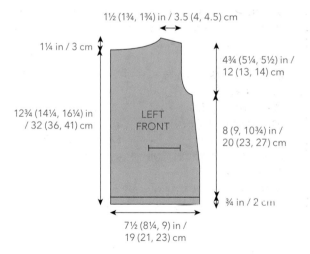

1½ (1¾, 1¾) in / 3.5 (4, 4.5) cm

1¼ in / 3 cm

4¾ (5¼, 5½) in / 12 (13, 14) cm

12¾ (14¼, 16¼) in / 32 (36, 41) cm

LEFT FRONT

8 (9, 10¾) in / 20 (23, 27) cm

¾ in / 2 cm

7½ (8¼, 9) in / 19 (21, 23) cm

Coat (cont.)

Sleeves: With smaller needles, CO 30 (32, 34) sts and work in k1, p1 ribbing for ¾ in / 2 cm. Change to larger needles and continue as follows: purl 1 row on WS of work, *p 1 row on RS, k 1 row on WS, work 4 rows St st*; repeat 5 (6, 7) times. Finish in St st. *At the same time*, increase 1 st at each side every 6th (7th, 7th) row 4 (5, 6) times = 38 (42, 46) sts. When piece measures 5½ (7, 8) in / 14 (18, 20) cm, BO at each side every other row as follows: 5 sts, 4 sts, 3 sts and 2 sts. BO rem sts.

FINISHING

Front Bands (work both alike): With smaller needles, pick up and knit 52 (58, 66) sts along front edge. Work 4 rows of garter st and BO. Sew down the pocket linings, and seam shoulders.

Collar: With smaller needles, pick up and knit 66 (70, 74) sts around the neck. Work in k2, p2 ribbing for ¾ in / 2 cm, beginning and ending with p2 on the WS. Bind off.
Sew in the sleeves and sew the sleeve and side seams. Sew on the buttons.

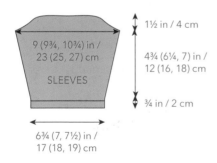

9 (9¾, 10¾) in / 23 (25, 27) cm

SLEEVES

1½ in / 4 cm

4¾ (6¼, 7) in / 12 (16, 18) cm

¾ in / 2 cm

6¾ (7, 7½) in / 17 (18, 19) cm

57 - Boots

SIZE

1 to 3 months

MATERIALS

Yarn: CYCA #5, Phildar Partner 6 (50% Nylon, 25% Wool, and 25% Acrylic, 71 yd/65 m / 50 g), 1 ball Slate

Needles: U.S. sizes 7 and 8 / 4.5 and 5 mm; cable needle

Notions: Stitch holder

PATTERN STITCHES

-Ribbing: *K2, p2*.

-Garter stitch: Knit every row.

-Cable: Row 1: *P2, k3*. Row 2 and all even-numbered rows: work the sts as they present themselves. Row 3: *P2, slip 1 st to the cable needle and hold in front of work, k2, then k the st from the cable needle*. Repeat the 4 rows.

INSTRUCTIONS (MAKE 2 ALIKE)

The booties are begun at the top of the leg. Using larger needles, CO 32 sts. Work in cable pattern until piece measures 2¾ in / 7 cm. Slip the 11 sts at each side to a holder and work on the 10 center sts for the top of the foot for 1¾ in / 4 cm. Now work the 11 sts on hold at the right, pick up and knit 7 sts along selvedge at top of foot, work the 10 sts at the toe, pick up and knit 7 sts on the other top selvedge, then work the last 11 sts on hold. For the bootie foot, work 8 rows of garter st on the 46 sts and BO.

Sole: With smaller needles, CO 5 sts and work in garter st, increasing 1 st at each side on every other row 2 times. Knit without shaping for 2½ in / 6 cm; then BO 1 st at each side every other row 2 times. BO rem sts.

FINISHING

Seam the leg. Sew the foot around the sole, placing the back seam at the center of the sole cast-on row and the center of foot toe at center of sole bind-off row.

CABLES

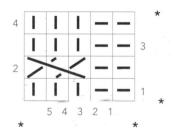

Repeat from * to *

| I | = Knit on RS, purl on WS

| — | = Purl on RS, knit on WS

= Slip 1 st to cable needle and hold in front of work.
K the next 2 sts, then knit the st on cable needle.

58 – Gray Sweater

This mini kimono-like wrap is made in stockinette stitch with a Liberty ribbon to tie it. Pilou yarn. U.S. size 8 / 5 mm needles.

59 – Booties

Lovely booties to match the sweater. Pilou yarn. U.S. size 8 / 5 mm needles.

60 - Plum Sweater

The same wrap, knit in a different yarn and closed with a satin ribbon. Phil Douce yarn. U.S. size 8 / 5 mm needles.

58 - Gray Sweater

SIZES

1 (3, 6) months

MATERIALS

Yarn: CYCA #2, Phildar Pilou (50% Acrylic, 29% Nylon, 13% Wool, and 8% Elasthan, 66 yd/60 m / 25 g), 4 (6, 6) balls Khaki or Denim

Needles: U.S. size 8 / 5 mm

Notions: 43¼ (47¼, 51¼) in / 110 (120, 130) cm of flowered cotton bias tape

GAUGE

24 sts and 38 rows in St st = 4 x 4 in / 10 x 10 cm. **Note:** The yarn is very stretchy. The swatch should be made several hours before measuring. Adjust needle size if necessary to obtain gauge.

PATTERN STITCHES

-Stockinette stitch: Knit on RS, purl on WS

-Double dec for the neck: At the beginning of the row, k1, k3tog, work to the end. At the end of the row, work to last 4 sts, k3tog, k1

INSTRUCTIONS

Back: CO 52 (56, 60) sts and work in St st. When piece measures 4¾ (5½, 6¼) in / 12 (14, 16) cm, shape armhole: at each side on every other row, BO 2 sts once and 1 st 3 times = 42 (46, 50) sts. When piece measures 8¼ (9½, 10¾) in / 21 (24, 27) cm, BO across, with a separate strand for each shoulder and the back neck: 10 (11, 12) sts for each shoulder and the 22 (24, 26) center sts for the neck.

Right Front: CO 45 (49, 53) sts and work in St st until piece measures 4 (4¾, 5½) in / 10 (12, 14) cm. Begin neck shaping at the right side as follows:

1 month: On every other row at neck edge, double dec 5 times; then *work 2 rows without shaping and work a double dec on every other row 2 times*; work * to * 5 times.

3 months: BO 3 sts once, then work a double dec once after 2 rows, *work 2 rows without shaping, work double dec every other row 2 times*; work * to * 7 times.

6 months: Work double dec every other row 8 times, *work 2 rows without shaping then work double dec every other row 2 times*; work * to * 5 times. *At the same time*, when piece measures 4¾ (5½, 6¼) in / 12 (14, 16) cm, shape armhole at left side as for back. When piece measures 8¼ (9½, 10¾) in / 21 (24, 27) cm, bind off rem 10 (11, 12) sts for shoulder.

Left Front: Work as for the right front, reversing all shaping.

Sleeves: CO 36 (38, 40) sts and work in St st for ⅜ in / 1 cm. Inc at each side as follows: 1 st every 7th row 5 times (1 st every 8th row 6 times; 1 st every 8th row 7 times) = 46 (50, 54) sts. When piece measures 4¼ (6, 6¾) in / 11 (15, 17) cm, at each side on every other row, BO 2 sts once and 1 st 3 times. Bind off rem sts.

FINISHING

Sew the shoulder seams. Attach sleeves. Sew the sleeve and side seams, leaving an opening of ⅜ in / 1 cm at the right side 3½ (4¼, 5¼) in / 9 (11, 13) cm from the bottom. Fold down the length of bias tape and pinch. Cut into 2 equal parts. Sew one piece at the point of each front to tie the sweater.

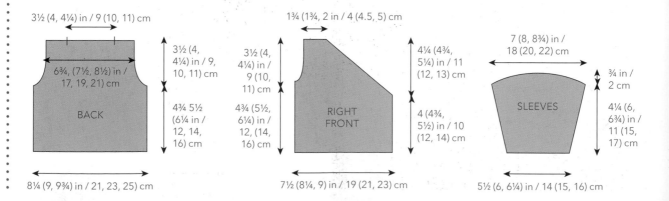

BACK — 3½ (4, 4¼) in / 9 (10, 11) cm — 6¾ (7½, 8½) in / 17, 19, 21) cm — 3½ (4, 4¼) in / 9, 10, 11) cm — 4¾ 5½ (6¼ in / 12, 14, 16) cm — 8¼ (9, 9¾) in / 21, 23, 25) cm

RIGHT FRONT — 1¾ (1¾, 2 in / 4 (4.5, 5) cm — 3½ (4, 4¼) in / 9 (10, 11) cm — 4¾ (5½, 6¼ in / 12, (14, 16) cm — 4¼ (4¾, 5¼) in / 11 (12, 13) cm — 4 (4¾, 5½) in / 10 (12, 14) cm — 7½ (8¼, 9) in / 19 (21, 23) cm

SLEEVES — 7 (8, 8¾) in / 18 (20, 22) cm — ¾ in / 2 cm — 4¼ (6, 6¾) in / 11 (15, 17) cm — 5½ (6, 6¼) in / 14 (15, 16) cm

59 - *Booties*

SIZE

1 to 3 months

MATERIALS

Yarn: CYCA #2, Phildar Pilou (50% Acrylic, 29% Nylon, 13% Wool, and 8% Elasthan, 66 yd/60 m / 25 g), 1 ball Khaki or Denim

Needles: U.S. size 8 / 5 mm

Notions: 15¾ in / 40 cm of flowered cotton bias tape; 2 buttons

GAUGE

24 sts and 38 rows in St st = 4 x 4 in / 10 x 10 cm. **Note:** The yarn is very stretchy. The swatch should be made several hours before measuring. Adjust needle size if necessary to obtain gauge.

PATTERN STITCHES

-Stockinette stitch: Knit on RS, purl on WS

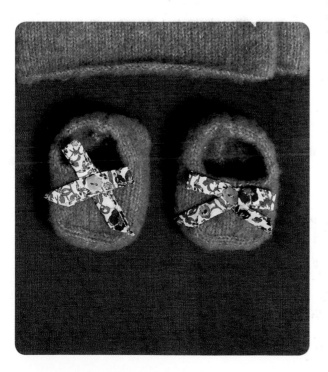

INSTRUCTIONS

The booties are made in one piece beginning at the center of the heel.
CO 10 sts and work in St st for ¾ in / 2 cm. CO 5 sts at the right side = 15 sts.
When piece measures 3 in / 7.5 cm, CO 5 sts at the left side = 20 sts.
When piece measures 3¾ in / 9.5 cm, BO 5 sts at each side and, when piece measures 5¼ in / 13.5 cm, CO 5 sts at each side.
When piece measures 6¼ in / 16 cm, BO 5 sts at the left side.
When piece measures 8¼ in / 21 cm, BO 5 sts at the right side.
When piece measures 9 in / 23 cm, BO all the sts.

FINISHING

Sew the top of the bootie, matching C and C together; then sew the toe at the top of the foot.
For the edge of the foot, pick up and knit 38 sts on C' and C'. Knit one row and BO.
Sew B and B together to close the sole; then sew the toe of the sole.
Sew A and A together to close the back.
Cut the bias tape into 2 pieces, each 8 in / 20 cm long. Fold the wrong sides tog. Stitch in place. Make a flat bow and attach one to the top of each bootie by sewing the button at the center.

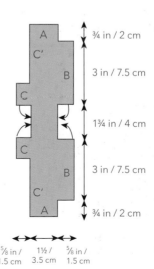

	¾ in / 2 cm
A	
C'	
B	3 in / 7.5 cm
C	1¾ in / 4 cm
C	
B	3 in / 7.5 cm
C'	
A	¾ in / 2 cm

⅝ in / 1.5 cm | 1½ / 3.5 cm | ⅝ in / 1.5 cm

60 - *Plum Sweater*

SIZES

1 (3, 6) months

MATERIALS

Yarn: CYCA #4, Phildar Phil Douce (100% Polyester, 94 yd/86 m / 50 g), 2 (3, 3) balls Heather

Needles: U.S. size 8 / 5 mm

Notions: satin ribbon ⅜ in / 1 cm wide and 43¼ (47¼, 51¼) in / 110 (120, 130) cm long

GAUGE

15 sts and 27 rows in St st = 4 x 4 in / 10 x 10 cm. Adjust needle size if necessary to obtain gauge.

PATTERN STITCHES

-Stockinette st: Knit on RS, purl on WS
-Double decrease for the neck: At the beginning of the row, k1, k3tog, work to the end. At the end of the row, work to last 4 sts, k3tog, k1.

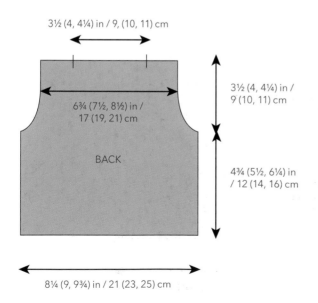

3½ (4, 4¼) in / 9, (10, 11) cm

6¾ (7½, 8½) in / 17 (19, 21) cm

3½ (4, 4¼) in / 9 (10, 11) cm

BACK

4¾ (5½, 6¼) in / 12 (14, 16) cm

8¼ (9, 9¾) in / 21 (23, 25) cm

INSTRUCTIONS

Back: CO 33 (36, 39) sts and work in St st until piece measures 4¾ (5½, 6¼) in / 12 (14, 16) cm.

Shape the armholes, binding off 1 st at each side on every other row 3 times = 27 (30, 33) sts.

When piece measures 8¼ (9½, 10¾) in / 21 (24, 27) cm, BO across, with a separate strand for each shoulder and the back neck: 7 (8, 9) sts at each side for the shoulders, and 13 (14, 15) sts at the center for back neck.

Right Front: CO 28 (31, 34) sts and work in St st until piece measures 4 (4¾, 5½) in / 10 (12, 14) cm. Shape the neck, binding off at the front edge on every other row as follows:

1 month: *On every 3rd row, double dec 3 times*; work * to * 2 times then, every 4th row, double dec 3 times = 18 sts decreased.

3 months: *On every 3rd row, double dec 3 times*; work * to * 2 times, then, on every 4th row, double dec 4 times = 20 sts decreased.

6 months: *On every 3rd row, double dec 3 times*; work * to * 3 times, then, on every 4th row, double dec 2 times = 22 sts decreased

At the same time, when piece measures 4¾ (5½, 6¼) in / 12 (14, 16) cm, at the left side, shape armhole as for back.

When piece measures 8¼ (9½, 10¾) in / 21 (24, 27) cm, BO the 7 (8, 9) shoulder sts.

Left Front: Work as for the right front, reversing all shaping.

Sleeves: CO 23 (24, 25) sts and work in St st for ⅜ in / 1 cm. Inc 1 st at each side as follows: every 8th row 3 times (every 9th row 4 times; every 8th row 5 times), then, when piece measures 4¼ (6, 6¾) in / 11 (15, 17) cm, bind off 1 st at each side 3 times on every other row. Bind off the rem sts.

FINISHING

Sew the shoulder seams. Attach sleeves. Sew the sleeve and side seams, leaving an opening of ⅜ in / 1 cm at the right side 3½ (4¼, 5¼) in / 9 (11, 13) cm from the bottom. Cut the ribbon into 2 equal lengths. Sew one piece to the point of each front for ties.

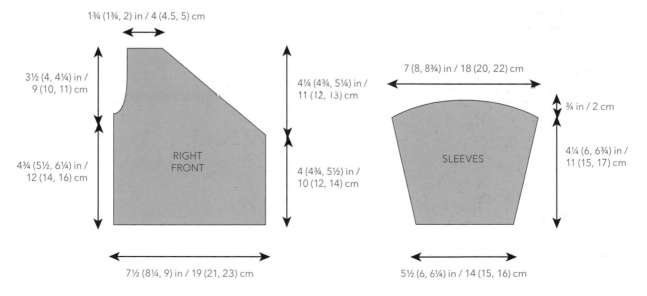

1¾ (1¾, 2) in / 4 (4.5, 5) cm

3½ (4, 4¼) in / 9 (10, 11) cm

4¾ (5½, 6¼) in / 12 (14, 16) cm

RIGHT FRONT

4¼ (4¾, 5¼) in / 11 (12, 13) cm

4 (4¾, 5½) in / 10 (12, 14) cm

7½ (8¼, 9) in / 19 (21, 23) cm

7 (8, 8¾) in / 18 (20, 22) cm

¾ in / 2 cm

SLEEVES

4¼ (6, 6¾) in / 11 (15, 17) cm

5½ (6, 6¼) in / 14 (15, 16) cm

61
Gray Blanket

Superb for the cradle or buggy, backed with Liberty fabric. Gray version. Stockinette stitch and squares of garter stitch. Partner 6 yarn. U.S. size 7 / 4.5 mm needles.

62 – *Plum Blanket*

The same blanket in plum, backed with a Liberty floral print.
Stockinette stitch and garter stitch squares. Partner 6 yarn.
U.S. size 7 / 4.5 mm needles.

61 & 62 - *Gray and Plum Blankets*

MATERIALS

Yarn: CYCA #5, Phildar Partner 6 (50% Nylon, 25% Wool, and 25% Acrylic, 71 yd/65 m / 50 g), 8 balls Aviator (gray blanket), 8 balls Mulberry (plum blanket)

Needles: U.S. sizes 7 / 4.5 mm

Notions: cotton fabric 25½ x 31½ in / 65 x 80 cm; matching sewing thread

GAUGE

18 sts and 26 rows in St st = 4 x 4 in / 10 x 10 cm. Adjust needle size if necessary to obtain gauge.

PATTERN STITCHES

-Stockinette stitch: Knit on RS, purl on WS

-Garter stitch: Knit every row

INSTRUCTIONS

CO 108 sts and work following the chart. Repeat the 54 chart sts 2 times for the width and repeat the 84 rows 2½ times for the length. BO.

Place the blanket and fabric with wrong sides facing. Fold the excess fabric to the inside between the 2 thicknesses and sew around with invisible stitches. Stitch through the 2 layers vertically and horizontally according to the chart.

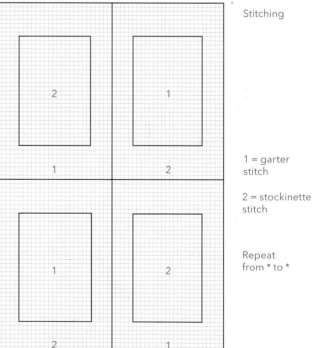

Stitching

1 = garter stitch

2 = stockinette stitch

Repeat from * to *

Stitching

Stitching

63
Hooded Coat

A magnificent hooded coat made with double cables and garter stitch. Quiétude yarn. U.S sizes 4 and 6 / 3.5 and 4 mm needles.

64 - *Mittens*

These mittens are joined with a long wool cord that can be passed through the coat to avoid mislaying them. Cables and garter stitch. Quiétude yarn. U.S. size 4 / 3.5 mm needles. A cable needle.

63 - *Hooded Coat*

SIZES

3 (6, 12) months

MATERIALS

Yarn: CYCA #4, Phildar Quiétude (50% Wool and 50% Acrylic, 98 yd/90 m / 50 g), 4 (5, 6) balls Neptune

Needles: U.S. sizes 4 and 6 / 3.5 and 4 mm; cable needle

Notions: 6 buttons

GAUGE

23 sts and 27 rows in pattern on larger needles = 4 x 4 in / 10 x 10 cm. Adjust needle sizes if necessary to obtain gauge.

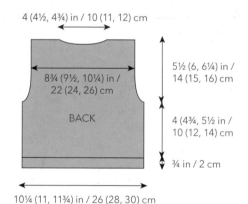

4 (4½, 4¾) in / 10 (11, 12) cm

8¾ (9½, 10¼) in / 22 (24, 26) cm

BACK

5½ (6, 6¼) in / 14 (15, 16) cm

4 (4¾, 5½) in / 10 (12, 14) cm

¾ in / 2 cm

10¼ (11, 11¾) in / 26 (28, 30) cm

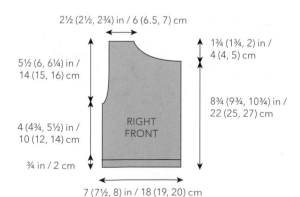

2½ (2½, 2¾) in / 6 (6.5, 7) cm

1¾ (1¾, 2) in / 4 (4, 5) cm

5½ (6, 6¼) in / 14 (15, 16) cm

RIGHT FRONT

8¾ (9¾, 10¾) in / 22 (25, 27) cm

4 (4¾, 5½) in / 10 (12, 14) cm

¾ in / 2 cm

7 (7½, 8) in / 18 (19, 20) cm

PATTERN STITCHES

-Garter stitch: Knit every row

-Stockinette stitch: *Knit on RS, purl on WS*

-Cable: Work the 12 sts of the chart, repeating the 8 rows

INSTRUCTIONS

Back: With smaller needles, CO 60 (66, 72) sts and work in garter st for ¾ in / 2 cm. Change to larger needles and continue as follows: work 7 (10, 13) sts in St st, *12 sts following the cable chart, 5 sts in garter st*; work * to * 2 times, then work 12 sts following the cable chart and 7 (10, 13) sts in St st. When piece measures 4¾ (5½, 6) in / 12 (14, 16) cm, shape armholes: at each side, on every other row, BO 3 sts once, 2 sts once, and one st once = 48 (54, 60) sts. When piece measures 9¾ (11, 12¼) in / 25 (28, 31) cm, BO the 12 (14, 16) center sts and finish each side separately. Work 2 rows and then BO 6 sts at neck edge. When piece measures 10¼ (11½, 12¾) in / 26 (29, 32) cm, BO rem 12 (14, 16) sts for shoulder. Work the other side the same way, reversing shaping.

Right Front: With smaller needles, CO 41 (44, 47) sts and work in garter st for ¾ in / 2 cm. Change to larger needles and continue as follows: work *5 sts in garter st, 12 sts following the cable chart*; work * to * 2 times, then work 7 (10, 13) sts in St st.

When piece measures 2½ (2¾, 3½) in / 6 (7, 9) cm, make a one-st buttonhole at the center of each garter st band; then make 2 more buttonholes, spaced 2¾ (3¼, 3¼) in / 7 (8, 8) cm apart.

When piece measures 4¾ (5½, 6) in / 12 (14, 16) cm, shape armhole at side: on every other row, BO 3 sts once, 2 sts once, and one st once = 35 (38, 41) sts.

When piece measures 8¾ (9¾, 10¾) in / 22 (25, 27) cm, shape the neck, binding off at neck edge on every other row: BO 9 (10, 11) sts once, 6 sts once, 5 sts once, 2 sts once and 1 st once.

When piece measures 10¼ (11½, 12¾) in / 26 (29, 32) cm, BO the 12 (14, 16) shoulder sts.

CABLE

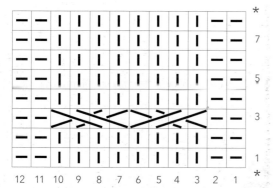

Repeat from * to *

⊡ = Knit on RS, purl on WS.

⊟ = Purl on RS, knit on WS

= Slip 2 sts to cable needle and hold in back of work. Knit the next 2 sts then knit the sts on cable needle. Slip 2 sts to cable needle and hold in front of work. Knit the next 2 sts then knit the sts on cable needle.

Hooded Coat (cont.)

Left Front: Work as for right front, reversing all shaping.

Sleeves: With smaller needles, CO 36 (38, 40) sts and work in garter st for ¾ in / 2 cm. Change to larger needles and continue as follows: work 12 (13, 14) sts in St st, 12 sts following the cable chart, 12 (13, 14) sts in St st. Inc 1 st at each side every 5 rows 7 (8, 9) times = 50 (54, 58) sts.
When piece measures 6 (6¾, 8) in / 15 (17, 20) cm, shape sleeve cap: at each side, on every other row, BO 3 sts 2 times, 2 sts 4 times, 1 st once. BO rem sts.

Hood: With smaller needles, CO 72 (78, 84) sts and work in garter st for ¾ in / 2 cm. Change to larger needles and continue as follows: work 30 (33, 36) sts in St st, 12 sts following the cable chart, 30 (33, 36) sts in St st.
When piece measures 5½ (6, 6¼) in / 14 (15, 16) cm, at each side, on every other row, BO 5 sts 5 times (6 sts 3 times and 5 sts 2 times; 6 sts 4 times and 7 sts once). Continue on the 22 center sts. BO rem sts when piece measures 11½ (12¼, 13) in / 29 (31, 33) cm.

FINISHING

Sew the shoulder seams. Attach sleeves. Sew the sleeve and side seams. Overlap the fronts and sew on the buttons to correspond to the buttonholes. Seam the back of the hood and sew it to the neck, from the center of one front to the center of the other.

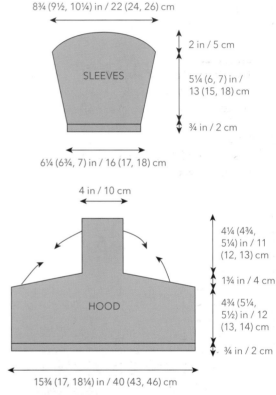

8¾ (9½, 10¼) in / 22 (24, 26) cm

SLEEVES

2 in / 5 cm

5¼ (6, 7) in / 13 (15, 18) cm

¾ in / 2 cm

6¼ (6¾, 7) in / 16 (17, 18) cm

4 in / 10 cm

HOOD

4¼ (4¾, 5¼) in / 11 (12, 13) cm

1¾ in / 4 cm

4¾ (5¼, 5½) in / 12 (13, 14) cm

¾ in / 2 cm

15¾ (17, 18¼) in / 40 (43, 46) cm

64 - *Mittens*

SIZES
3 to 6 months (6 to 12 months)

MATERIALS
Yarn: CYCA #4, Phildar Quiétude (50% Wool and 50% Acrylic, 98 yd/90 m / 50 g), 1 ball Neptune
Needles: U.S. size 6 / 4 mm; cable needle

GAUGE
23 sts and 27 rows in pattern = 4 x 4 in / 10 x 10 cm. Adjust needle size if necessary to obtain gauge.

CABLE

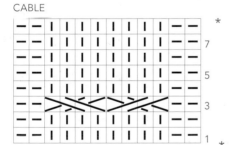

Repeat from * to *

☐ = Knit on the RS, purl on the WS

⊟ = Purl on the RS, knit on the WS

= Slip 2 sts to cable needle and hold in back of work. Knit the next 2 sts then knit the sts on cable needle. Slip 2 sts to cable needle and hold in front of work. Knit the next 2 sts then knit the sts on cable needle.

PATTERN STITCHES
-Garter stitch: Knit every row
-Stockinette stitch: Knit on RS, purl on WS
-Cable: Work the 12 sts of the chart, repeating the 8 rows

INSTRUCTIONS
CO 32 (36) sts, work in garter st for 2½ in / 6 cm, and then continue as follows: work 2 (3) sts in St st, 12 sts following the cable chart, 4 (6) sts in St st, 12 sts following the cable chart, 2 (3) sts in St st.
When piece measures 4¾ (5½) in / 12 (14) cm, divide work into 2 equal parts and work each side separately, decreasing 1 st at each side every other row 3 times. BO the 10 (12) rem sts.

FINISHING
Fold the mitten to sew the seam at the top and side. Fold up half the garter st to make a cuff. Make a twisted cord about 25½ / 65 cm long. Sew 1 end to the inside of each mitten.

Basic Information

The numbers for the smallest size are listed first and those for larger sizes are within parentheses. If only one number is given, it applies to all sizes.

INCREASES

Unless otherwise specified, increase with k1f&b (knit into front and then back of same stitch) or with M1. For a right–leaning increase, M1R, use left needle tip to lift strand between 2 sts from back to front and knit into front loop. For a left-leaning increase, M1L, use left needle tip to lift strand between 2 sts from front to back and knit into back loop. For increases across a row, use M1L. If you want mirror-image increases at the edges of piece, use M1R at beginning of row and M1L at end on RS.

SHORT ROWS

If working in garter stitch, you do not need to wrap stitches when working short rows.

If you wish to avoid holes when working short rows in stockinette, work specified number of stitches, then, with yarn behind, slip next st purlwise to right needle, bring yarn to front and slip st back to left needle; turn. When you once again work over all the sts on the row, knit or purl the wrap with the stitch it wraps. There are several methods for working short rows so check the internet or basic knitting books for additional information.

BUTTONHOLES

1-st buttonholes: K2tog (or p2tog on WS), yo.2-st buttonholes: BO 2 sts and, on following row, CO 2 sts over gap
OR K2tog, yo twice, ssk. On following row, knit and then purl into double yarnover.

Abbreviations

beg	begin(ning)	**mm**	millimeter(s)
BO	bind off (British cast off)	**p**	purl
ch	chain	**pm**	place marker
cm	centimeter(s)	**psso**	pass slipped st(s) over
cn	cable needle	**rem**	remain(s) (ing)
CO	cast on	**rnd(s)**	round(s)
dc	double crochet	**RS**	right side
dec	decrease	**sc**	single crochet
dpn	double pointed needles	**ssk**	slip, slip, knit: slip 1 st as if to knit, slip another st as if to knit; k together through back loops
g	gram(s)		
gauge	British tension		
in	inch (es)	**sl**	slip
inc	increase	**st(s)**	stitch(es)
k	knit	**St st**	stockinette stitch (British stocking st)
k2tog	knit 2 together		
M1	lifted increase (see Basic Information above)	**WS**	wrong side
		yd	yard(s)
m	meter(s)	**yo**	yarnover

Yarn Information

Webs – America's Yarn Store
75 Service Center Road
Northampton, MA 01060
800-367-9327
www.yarn.com
customerservice@yarn.com

Phildar Yarn Company
www.phildar.fr

If you are unable to obtain any of the yarn used in this book, it can be replaced with a yarn of a similar weight and composition. Please note, however, the finished projects may vary slightly from those shown, depending on the yarn used.

For more information on selecting or substituting yarn contact your local yarn shop or an online store, they are familiar with all types of yarns and would be happy to help you. Additionally, the online knitting community at Ravelry.com has forums where you can post questions about specific yarns. Yarns come and go so quickly these days and there are so many beautiful yarns available.